Becoming
A BADASS MEDITATOR

The 'Must-Know', 'Must-Have', and 'Must-Do'

Becoming A BADASS MEDITATOR

The 'Must-Know', 'Must-Have', and 'Must-Do'

AUTHOR'S CHANNEL

Find Deep Healing, Transform Your Life, and
Embrace the Unstoppable You

DR. RENU KHETAN

First edition 2023

The Author has made every effort to trace and acknowledge sources/ resources/individuals. In the event that any images/information have been incorrectly attributed or credited, the Author will be pleased to rectify these omissions at the earliest opportunity.

ISBN: 978-93-92546-24-2

Published by

AUTHOR'S CHANNEL

108, 1st floor, 3rd cross, 3rd stage, 8th Main,
Pillanna Garden, Bangalore 560045

http://authorschannel.in/

Strength from Earth,

Dreams from stars,

Fire from sun,

Wings from wind.

The sea of love is a reflection of the sky in the heart,

And the colours from the rainbows.

It's me in the Universe,

And the Universe in me.

- 'Mind Magic,'

Renu Khetan

CONTENTS

PREFACE

In a world where relentless demands prevail, the pursuit of profound rest and a happier existence have fast become humanity's deepest desires.

And there's one, scientifically proven way to achieve this vision; through meditation. Meditative practices have been sought after and mastered by thousands of people over thousands of years to guide them through chaos and restore a sense of balance. But it isn't just ancient wisdom that advocates for meditation. Through extensive research, countless twenty-first-century neuroscientists and psychologists are contributing an increasingly overwhelming amount of compelling evidence of its transformative power over the mind and body. Notably, some of the world's highest achievers have integrated meditation into their daily routines, contributing to their remarkable accomplishments in the athletic, creative, and musical arenas to name a few.

It's fascinating to witness how meditation intersects with the diverse fields of psychology, neuroscience, philosophy, performance enhancement, and personal development, showcasing its cutting-edge applications beyond tradition.

Meditation, much like medication, can be extremely healing, taking us from the depth of despair to the heights of mental health. However, let's not limit the value of meditation to challenging times alone. It holds equal importance during periods of success and abundance, allowing us to tap into sustainable inner reservoirs of peace, strength, and joy.

The world, it seems, is in increasing need of light. It is through meditation that I have discovered my own. After decades of working towards decoding the mysteries behind meditation, as well as cultivating a powerful daily practice, it is my intention to bring forth a new perspective on the topic. In "Becoming a Badass Meditator," I share my personal odyssey from struggle to serenity through experimental explorations of meditation with the hope of inspiring you to embark on your own journey. I passionately endeavour to help you ignite your own light, as I did, as well as confirm the following truth: everything you are ever going to need is already inside of you. As a health professional in the field of modern medicine with Indian heritage, it was deeply important to me to combine science with tradition to showcase the undeniable value of meditation to the world, and, of course, show you how to do it.

Within the pages of the book you're about to read, you will be provided with tools and instructions that are both clear and flexible, and thoroughly tried and tested. Together, we will overcome the obstacles and remove the stigma from meditation, breaking down the walls of misconception to reveal its true essence. In my experience, there is nothing that serves us on our journey towards a happier and more fulfilling existence than meditation. And you're about to see how accessible and enjoyable the experience can truly be.

This book is divided into three overarching sections: the "Must-Know", the "Must-Have", and the "Must-Do" of meditation.

The "Must-Know" section beautifully unravels the science behind meditation, connecting the intricate dots between the mind, body, spirit, and universe. Extensive research has revealed how meditation reshapes the structure, chemistry, and activity of our brains, unlocking extraordinary, altered states of mind that tap into higher faculties like creativity and problem-solving. Meditation can connect us to universal consciousness, harnessing the principles of quantum mechanics to attract our true desires in life. Innovative techniques such as biofeedback, virtual reality, and brainwave entrainment provide valuable insights into the impact of meditation on the human mind, and therefore, the physical body to which it is intrinsically linked. Knowing how powerful meditation is on a cognitive level enriches the experience and solidifies our faith in the process, motivating us to commit to a regular practice to gain mastery.

The "Must-Have" section of the book offers practical advice on creating a conducive environment for meditation and developing a powerful habit that sticks.

In the "Must-Do" section, the real work begins. Applying the knowledge gained, you'll embark on three easy yet powerful steps to prepare for meditation. These steps set the foundation for eight clear and transformative foundational meditation practices, the 'meditation ladder', allowing you to harness deep rest, experience healing, redefine your self-image, and tap into your limitless potential.

Whether you're a novice or a seasoned practitioner, this book will elevate your meditation practice to unprecedented levels of effectiveness. Approach it with an open mind, release conditioned beliefs, and bear witness to the metamorphosis occurring within you.

"Becoming a Badass Meditator" serves as the perfect recipe to become a badass not only during the meditation itself but also in your ability to change your own reality. Through meditation, we remain connected to our inner power, manifest our goals with unwavering clarity and focus, and live a life resonating with the rhythm of true fulfilment.

This book is a heartfelt compilation of insights drawn from years of my passionate practice, interwoven with innovative ideas that resonate with the urgent needs of our time. I have not originated anything; instead, I've curated and connected existing wisdom with science, transforming it into an actionable framework.

It is my belief that "Becoming a Badass Meditator" is more than just a book; it's a compass, one that will guide you towards your true self—a self that is peaceful, strong, and joyous.

Chapter 1

My Quest to Become a Badass Meditator

"The wound is the place where the Light enters you."

- Rumi

Without meditation, only God knows what kind of person I'd be. As well as being a passionate homemaker, closely knitted with my husband and two beautiful boys, I'm also a full-time health professional, dedicating most of my waking moments to working as a child specialist. Although nothing brings me more contentment than the warmth and comfort of my family, and although I generally enjoy my job, from the outside, I live a 'stressful' life. Like many others, I am constantly challenged to balance the demands of work, family, and self-care.

It would be impossible to do this, and do this with a smile on my face, without the secret, wholesome weapon that is meditation. Meditation is my sanctuary; my place of solace. It provides me with the sanity I need to navigate the relentless pressures of work, the daily emotional wear and tear of being a mum, and the pursuit of work-life balance. It is meditation, and meditation alone, that has reduced my stress and anxiety while nurturing an elevated level of resilience. Through meditation, I gain clarity, self-awareness, self-acceptance, and emotional regulation, enriching my experiences and relationships. It helps me release mental and emotional wounds, facilitating unexplainable healing and transforming seemingly impossible difficulties into opportunities.

I am continually amazed by the power of meditation to unlock my boundless potential as a human being.

Meditation became a game changer for me, although it didn't happen overnight. It required trust, patience, commitment, self-honesty and study. It took me a considerable amount of time to grasp this fundamental truth. This book is an accumulation of everything I learned.

My journey in meditation, despite my Indian heritage, (India, if you didn't already know, was the birthplace of meditation), didn't begin until I moved to the UK in my late twenties. My life in India was not always sunshine and roses growing up, you see, at least, that's how I perceived it. Due to our parent's loving resilience, my father's strong work ethic and my mother's strength and affection, me, my brother and my sister, were able to liberally spread our wings under their seen and unseen struggles. Despite the normal challenges of youth, their love and support shielded us from the harshness of life.

A couple of years before I moved to the UK, I found myself studying to become a doctor. Life was going well. I worked hard to excel in my studies, made lasting friendships, and looked forward to a promising future. After graduating, I moved to Mumbai to pursue specialised training as a child specialist at a prestigious institute. It was this phase that brought new, unforeseen challenges into my life. Needless to say, it was a huge wake-up call when the harsh realities of life hit me, prompting a deep examination of my true self.

Until then, I'd lived most of my life in a small town away from the bustling streets of the city. This meant I had zero street smarts, rendering me vulnerable to being manipulated. All I knew was the value of putting my head down and working hard, but upon comparing myself to other 'city people,' my resilience was on the low side, and my skin wasn't nearly as thick as theirs. My financial life was also very challenging, as I struggled to make ends meet with the limited income I received from the hospital. Within the chaos, it was during this time that my father was diagnosed with terminal cancer. I felt completely shattered emotionally, mentally, physically, and financially.

By the time I got to the UK to pursue my career as a child specialist, I was exhausted. The move in and of itself exhausted me even more. Once again, I found myself starting from scratch, adapting to a new culture and work environment. As someone who had always been an exceptional student, my confidence was (initially) high. However, a few months down the road, this new country made me feel unworthy and I began to doubt my abilities. I developed a poor self-image and very low self-esteem, which led to feelings of powerlessness, difficulty expressing myself, and an inability to assert my own beliefs. I was afraid of making mistakes and being rejected, rendering me desperate for external validation. I felt inexplicably unsupported and lonely. All these emotions contributed to anxiety, clouded thinking, indecisiveness, and ultimately, unsatisfactory advances at work. I was falling apart, but I had no idea how to help myself. I even lacked the knowledge and tools to identify what exactly was wrong in the first place and what I needed to move forward.

My brother noticed my struggle, and, with hopes of helping me, introduced me to the Art of Living Foundation (AoL); a non-profit organisation founded by spiritual leader Sri Sri Ravi Shankar. The foundation offered various workshops and courses that incorporated techniques such as breathing exercises (Sudarshan Kriya), meditation, yoga, and practical wisdom to help individuals manage stress, improve mental clarity, and foster a sense of inner peace and harmony. I decided to give it a try, starting with meditation. At first, I had no idea how meditation would help me, and was resistant to the idea that it could help bring stability to my whirlwind of a life. After all, it was just sitting on your butt and closing your eyes, right? How could that possibly have any effect on real-world problems? That said, I persevered. Although my meditation practice was far from perfect, notably inconsistent, filled with doubts, procrastination, and a lack of proper technique, it did indeed help.

Since the beginning of my meditation journey, I obtained several degrees from the Royal College of Paediatrics in the UK, including MRCPCH and FRCPCH. I eventually became a Consultant in Paediatrics in the NHS, which had been my aspiration for years. Life continued moving forward, and I carried on meditating, unaware that it had had any other benefits apart from short-term relaxation. I had completely missed the correlation between my professional success and my meditation practice. And yet, I had only scratched the surface of meditation.

A few years down the road, I'd managed to hit all my professional goals. I had the 'dream' job my parents would be proud of. I had a healthy family. Yet I was suffocating. The grind of the 9-5, the monotony of my life, and the dysfunctionality of the system I was working in was killing me. This led to more anxiety, fear, uncertainty, and self-sabotaging behaviours, creating a negative spiral that seemed never-ending. I pleaded with the heavens for a change, to break free from the bondage of the life I thought I wanted. I didn't exactly know what my *actual* dream life looked like, but it wasn't this. All I knew was that I wanted to escape from where I was.

Miraculously, my prayers were answered in a very unexpected way. As they say, "The teacher comes when the student is ready!" And my teacher was the COVID-19 pandemic. Of course, bearing witness to the daily news from 10 Downing Street, the reports of deaths, lack of resources, overwhelmed hospitals (I was working in one), constantly changing guidelines, international comparisons, and quarantine measures were awful. The world felt incredibly uncertain and miserable for most. Despite this, it was during this time that I had the opportunity to be truly present at home, appreciating the simple joys of life—food, music, my children, birdsong, the seasons and the night sky. All of this inspired me to meditate again, but this time, dive deeper into the practice. Not only did it allow me to appreciate the simple pleasures of life I just described, but it also protected me against the new, unprecedented stress at work caused by the pandemic.

My meditation practice combined with the pandemic also gave me the gift of heightened appreciation, as did the rest of the country. In order to give thanks to those working on the frontline in the NHS, the British public would open their doors and clap and cheer every evening at 8pm for us. They also honoured us by putting up huge symbolic rainbows on their windows and garden fences as a sign of hope, often painted by children and a shaky 'THANK YOU, NHS!' underneath. I got involved myself, grabbing watercolours from my son's room and painting rainbows on my backyard fence. I ran out of colours and ordered more. Painting rainbows brought me indescribable joy.

As I continued with the 'online morning healer meditations' (more on that later), my artistic side began to flourish alongside them. It amazed me how my life had started to transform, and I slowly began to notice the correlation between meditation and my day-to-day levels of contentment. I took meditation seriously, practising it twice a day, and as a result, my creativity sparked, and I gained new insights about who I was and what I wanted. I even took on a 21-day manifestation challenge, which opened doors to self-development programs that had a profound impact on me. I was exposed to countless "aha" moments and my brain eagerly soaked up all the new information. From someone who rarely reads books, I found myself devouring them to gratefully apply the teachings to my life. Among them, were books about the hard science behind meditation, which solidified my practice and my faith that this healing modality was actually working.

My artwork got better and better, and the time I spent painting increased. As I painted, my head began to align with my heart, allowing me to enter a deep state of flow, much like I did when I meditated. I finally started feeling fulfilled; a state I had always wanted to be in.

Now, meditation is no longer a chore for me, nor does it require any special effort. My brain has been so strongly rewired and reprogrammed that I wake up, sit on my bed, put on my AirPods, and immediately start meditating as naturally as I'd make a cup of tea. I know exactly which meditation to practise based on my state of mind. If my thoughts are overwhelming or I feel restless, I focus on grounding myself. On peaceful days, I visualise my dreams, and on other tougher days, I surrender and seek higher guidance. My self-image, self-confidence, and self-esteem have dramatically changed. Once an emotionally sensitive person, I have become emotionally empowered. I have become more efficient and focused. My awareness has sharpened. I am making the right choices, better decisions, and thus better results. Suddenly, I feel that I have more time on my hands. I complete tasks in half the time it used to take me, using the remaining time to cultivate my mind. I enjoy waking up with an inner calling to carry out my rituals, knowing that they set the tone for a better day.

I couldn't imagine not doing these practices, as I'm aware of their positive impact on my overall well-being. Because of this, I felt a strong urge to share my experiences with the world, hence why I started writing about it. And you now hold my book in your hands.

KEY POINTS:

1. Meditation is a powerful tool for personal transformation.

2. Practice meditation with dedication and commitment and within very little time, you'll start seeing profound results.

3. Meditation can be used as your shield against adversity as well as a catalyst for joy.

SOUL WORK:

1. Take out your journal and write your own life story. Try to keep it to a few pages. Cover your highs and lows.

2. Take the time to reflect on your past and examine the ways it impacted you as a person.

3. Identify some potential blocks and obstacles that are holding you back from living the life you desire, or feeling the way you wish to feel.

4. Reflect: Are you ready and committed to embracing meditation as a means to overcome these blocks?

Chapter 2

Meditation 101:The Why, What, Who and How

"Meditation is a journey from sound to silence, open to all who seek wisdom. It's about filling the mind with awareness, not perfect technique but perfect presence. In a gentle dance with yourself, there are no failures, only lessons. It's the bridge between who you think you are and who you truly are."

- Renu Khetan

In this chapter, we delve into the profound essence of meditation and its life-changing potential: the *why*, the *what*, the *who* and the *how*. Once you understand these four principles, you're ready to dive in.

WHY SHOULD WE MEDITATE?

There are many reasons that each and everyone should be practising meditation on a daily basis beyond the classic 'because it's relaxing' stereotype. Here are a few of the reasons that inspired me to deepen my practice.

You have the opportunity to be your true self: With meditation, you are given the chance to return to your core state of love and joy. Before coming into this world, we experienced a state of comfort while floating happily in our mother's womb. Having felt that comfort, we naturally crave to return to that state of being where we belong. Just as everything in the universe cycles back to its source, meditation serves as the medium that brings us back to our own. It trains the brain to recycle external impressions, redirect thoughts, look inward, promote a state of calm and clarity, and facilitate transformation—a journey that will 'bring you home.'.

You can rebel against the stress of modern life:

In today's modern world, filled with unrealistic expectations from those who surround us, we are constantly pushing ourselves to run ever more quickly on the treadmill of life. This causes a significant incoherence between the head and heart that knocks us off balance, often leading to chronic unhappiness. When we meditate, we reconnect with our minds and bodies as we slow down to a more natural rhythm of life. Through meditation, a deep sense of calm and perspective is gained.

You facilitate your self-confidence and self-love:

Our thoughts, actions, beliefs, and self-perception shape our experience of life. Past experiences and traumas can erode our self-esteem, self-image, and self-confidence, blocking our path to happiness and success. This results in fear, anxiety, uncertainty, anger, lack, unworthiness, doubts, and a host of negative emotions. To recycle these emotions, we must reconnect with compassion for ourselves, and meditation is the perfect starting point. By working with our inner belief systems, meditation gives us the quiet space to observe our inner chatter and change negative beliefs about ourselves to positive ones. And as we begin to treat ourselves with more love, we'll be more likely to treat others with the same level of compassion too.

You kickstart your own healing:

Whether physical or mental, the primary outcome of meditation is healing. When we sit in meditation, we begin to address past emotional, physical, and psychological wounds. Past wounds are healed by observing and becoming aware of the experiences, gaining clarity and perspective, i.e., cognitive reframing and emotional regulation. This helps in developing neuroplasticity; in other words, meditation gives you the keys to rewiring your brain.

A reprogrammed and healed brain is receptive to new insights and ideas which in turn is a fertile ground for transformation. We become more aware of our choices and decisions, and live life from a place of calm and centredness, as opposed to our hurt inner children.

You are given the chance to take control over your life:

A healed, and transformed person has the ability to consciously create and attract desired outcomes and experiences into their life. It involves setting clear intentions, aligning your thoughts and emotions with those intentions, and taking inspired action. Manifestation practices include visualisation meditations, affirmations, and cultivating a positive mindset.

From healing, transformation, and manifestation, meditation quite literally brings about a new reality for the meditator.

WHAT IS MEDITATION?

Meditation goes far beyond sitting still and closing our eyes, although of course this is involved. It also goes beyond the concept of mindfulness, a state of awareness that involves bringing one's attention to the present moment without judgement.

Let us explore the original concept of meditation itself. Meditation is known as "Dhyana" in Sanskrit, meaning contemplation, self-reflection, healing, and personal growth. By diving deep into introspection, we can observe our thoughts, emotions, and limiting factors. By merely observing, we begin to think from the neocortex, which helps to gain clarity and perspective which in turn helps to dissipate negative energies and gives our bodies permission to heal and relax. This helps to shed old masks that no longer serve us, enabling us to nourish our true selves.

Meditation can be compared to tending a garden. Just as weeds need to be removed and rocks need to be cleared for flowers to bloom, conscious decisions and preparations are necessary. Meditation nurtures our minds by eliminating the weeds and psychological obstacles, creating a fertile ground for growth. This allows our full potential to blossom. Meditation opens the door to abundance, success, and happiness. It is both self love and self care.

The Meditation Ladder

Meditation also offers a diverse range of possibilities and experiences. There are various types of meditations available to choose from, each serving a specific purpose and contributing to a comprehensive practice. These meditations are as follows: breathing meditations, body scan meditations, walking or dancing meditations, Chakra meditations, vipassana meditations, transcendental meditations, Mantra meditations, loving-kindness meditations, and visualisation meditations.

For any meditation, there are a series of phases to pass through before sinking into deep states of introspection. The foundational or core elements of meditation discussed in this book are akin to climbing a ladder, with each step representing a foundational element. Just like you can't reach the top of the ladder without stepping on the lower rungs first, you need to go through each foundational element to build a strong and immersive meditation experience. Each step prepares you for the next, and skipping a step might make the journey less fulfilling. Diagram 2a in the illustration section of the book shows the meditation ladder.

Think of the meditation ladder as the basic framework or skeleton of a building. It's the step-by-step process that guides you through different stages of meditation, from focusing on your breath to visualising your goals. Each step on the ladder represents a foundational element that helps you build a strong and effective meditation practice. They form the core structure of your meditation practice.

Now, imagine the different types of meditation as the unique decorations, furnishings, and features that you add to each floor in the building. These specific meditation practices add character, style, and functionality to each step on the ladder. They make the basic structure more engaging, personalised, and suitable for your individual needs.

THE 8 FOUNDATIONAL OR CORE STEPS OF THE MEDITATION LADDER ARE:

Step #1: Breathing (Breath Focus and Sense Sync)

Breathing is the first step of the ladder. Just like breathing is the foundation of life, it's also the foundation of meditation. Just as you need a stable base for the ladder, focusing on your breath helps you stabilise your mind and makes it easier to concentrate and stay present in the moment. Many people choose to simply observe the natural breathing pattern (mindful breathing), whereas others choose to elongate the breath to a specific rhythm (like in box breathing, where meditators breathe in for the count of four, hold for the count of four, exhale for the count of four and hold for the count of four).

Focusing on the breath and achieving a relaxed state can trigger the release of neurotransmitters like dopamine and endorphins, promoting a sense of well-being and reducing stress-related chemicals like cortisol. Regularly practising breath-focused meditation can lead to strengthening connections between brain regions involved in attention and emotional regulation.[1] Over time, increased grey matter density has been observed in brain areas associated with attention and self-awareness, like the prefrontal cortex, due to breath-awareness meditation.[2]

Step #2: Physical relaxation:

Once your mind is more centred, it's time to connect with your body. Physical relaxation is like a mental body check-up, making you aware of any tension and, in turn, releasing it. A common place to hold tension is within the shoulders, which are usually the first area to soften as we begin to meditate. People engage in physical relaxation through progressive muscle relaxation, body awareness and body scan meditations, where the meditator moves their awareness from the top of the head to the tips of the toes, relaxing muscle groups as they go.

Body scan meditations have been proven to activate the body's parasympathetic nervous system, leading to reduced levels of stress hormones and increased levels

---

1National Library of Medicine, Effects of Meditation Experience on Functional Connectivity of Distributed Brain Networks https://www.ncbi.nlm.nih.gov/pmc/articles/PMC3290768/

2National Library of Medicine, Increased dopamine tone during meditation-induced change of consciousness https://pubmed.ncbi.nlm.nih.gov/11958969/

of relaxation-inducing neurotransmitters[3]. This practice can promote the formation of new neural connections between brain regions involved in body awareness, leading to enhanced interoceptive abilities. Practising body scan meditations may lead to structural changes in brain regions associated with body perception, such as the insular cortex and somatosensory cortex, quite literally strengthening the connection between the mind and the body.[4]

Step #3: Mental relaxation:

Now that your body is relaxed, it's time to quiet the mental chatter. Mental relaxation helps reduce stress and anxiety, making your mind more receptive. A wonderful way to do this is to focus your attention on loving-kindness (basically wishing yourself and others well) or enjoy guided imagery (for example, focusing your mind's eye on tranquil, natural scenes such as a forest or a beach).

Achieving a mentally relaxed state can trigger the release of neurotransmitters like gamma-aminobutyric acid (GABA), which has calming effects on the brain. Regular mental relaxation may lead to increased neural

---

3 National Library of Medicine, Mindfulness, Interoception, and the Body: A Contemporary Perspective
https://www.ncbi.nlm.nih.gov/pmc/articles/PMC6753170/
4 National Library of Medicine, Mindfulness practice leads to increases in regional brain gray matter density
https://www.ncbi.nlm.nih.gov/pmc/articles/PMC3004979/

connectivity between the amygdala (emotion centre) and prefrontal cortex (executive control), promoting better emotional regulation. Prolonged mental relaxation has been associated with alterations in brain structure, including changes in the hippocampus related to memory and learning[5].

Step #4: Awareness stretching:

'Stretching' your awareness means expanding your focus beyond just your body. This step enhances mindfulness, helping you observe the space surrounding you and the sounds within it. Once your awareness is stretched, you may observe your thoughts and emotions as if from afar, without judgement. These are deeper and healthier states of mind. We cultivate this through mindfulness practices and non-reactive awareness states, also known as 'vipassana,' allowing you to perceive the true nature of reality and your authentic self (ever-changing).

Practising mindfulness and stretching awareness may increase serotonin levels, which are associated with improved mood and well-being. Mindfulness can enhance synaptic plasticity, facilitating the rewiring of neural circuits and promoting adaptive changes in the brain. Mindfulness meditation has been linked to increased grey matter volume in brain regions involved

---

5 National Library of Medicine, Meditation and Yoga can Modulate Brain Mechanisms that affect Behavior and Anxiety-A Modern Scientific Perspective https://www.ncbi.nlm.nih.gov/pmc/articles/PMC4769029/

in attention, such as the anterior cingulate cortex and hippocampus[6].

Step #5: Running Energy:

In this step, you learn to harness and direct your energy through movement of some kind. Running energy meditations boost vitality and spiritual connection.

Techniques like Qi Gong[7] (slow, controlled sequences of movements similar to Tai Qi) or Reiki (like a non-contact massage that channels universal life energy) have been associated with changes in neurotransmitters, including increased serotonin and endorphins, contributing to enhanced relaxation and energy flow.[8] Running energy practices may stimulate neural plasticity, influencing the organisation of neural networks associated with the regulation of energy and vitality.

A 'chakra meditation' is another example of an energy exercise, involving running energy through the body's

---

6 National Library of Medicine, Mindfulness practice leads to increases in regional brain gray matter density
https://www.ncbi.nlm.nih.gov/pmc/articles/PMC3004979/

7 National Library of Medicine, A comprehensive review of health benefits of qigong and tai chi
https://pubmed.ncbi.nlm.nih.gov/20594090/

8 National Library of Medicine,Does Reiki Benefit Mental Health Symptoms Above Placebo?
https://www.ncbi.nlm.nih.gov/pmc/articles/PMC9326483/

energy centres, aka chakras, therefore aligning them and clearing blockages.

Step #6: Grounding and letting go:

Now that you have a better handle on your energy, it's time to ground any negative emotions. Deep introspection and letting go encourage presence and self-reflection. By observing our thoughts, feelings, and sensations without judgement, we cultivate awareness and compassion. This helps with clarity of thought and the ability to make better choices and decisions. This step helps you find stability and overall emotional balance. Types of meditation in this arena include the RAIN approach (Recognize, Allow, Investigate, Nurture) or an emotional release meditation. To take this a step further, transcendental meditations can be used here to take us into higher states of consciousness, far beyond the constraints of negative emotions. More on this later.

These different approaches to deep introspection are tied to the Default Mode Network (DMN) in the brain (a network of interconnected brain regions that are active when an individual is not engaged in any specific task or external focus), which is vital when it comes to having a strong sense of self.

Regular meditation can increase control over the prefrontal cortex (involved in attention regulation), the anterior cingulate cortex (helps in resolving cognitive conflicts), and the amygdala (emotional processing), leading to reduced emotional reactivity and distraction.

Step #7: Creative Visualisation:

With a clear mind and balanced emotions, you are ready to immerse yourself in the world of visualisation. Visualisation involves creating images or scenarios in your 'mind's eye.' Creative visualisation is a mental technique that uses the imagination to create a mental image or scenario of what you want to manifest or achieve. This technique may also be used, however, in manifestation. Having video images of who we want to be and what we want to achieve helps bring clarity and speeds up the process of manifestation. To do this, we simply begin to imagine, as vividly as we can, our dreams as if they were already a reality. Types of meditation used in this step are 'Three Scene' technique and 'Mental video' technique.

Creative visualisation is like using your brain's visual cortex (picture-making part) to make imagined images feel real. It taps into the limbic system (emotion centre) of your brain to help you feel motivated. By imagining the same thing repeatedly, you're using the brain's ability to change and grow (neuroplasticity) to form new pathways, training it to recognize what you want. There's a special part of the brain called the RAS (Reticular Activating System) that helps focus your attention on your goals, letting you spot opportunities you might have missed otherwise. Visualisation also talks to the subconscious (automatic part) of your mind, causing you to act in ways that line up with your goals. It can even make your brain release like dopamine (happy chemicals), reinforcing positive feelings. Finally, your brain might treat what you're vividly imagining as real, which can help you feel relaxed physically. It's like your mind's way of practising for success!

Step #8: Mental Rehearsal:

A slightly different angle to visualisation is using it as a 'mental rehearsal.' This involves vividly visualising and practising skills or actions in preparation for an event. This is a common technique used by athletes, musicians, and other performers to enhance performance. Type of meditation used in this arena is Mental Rehearsal Technique'.

Mental rehearsal is a complex process involving multiple brain areas and networks responsible for motor planning and execution, spatial navigation, and higher cognitive functions. It's an effective strategy to mentally train the individual for whatever event lies ahead by harnessing the brain's plasticity and the overlap between cognitive and motor networks.

Remember, each step in the ladder is essential, and you can't skip any of them. Just as the lower rungs support your climb to the top, each foundational element of meditation prepares your mind for the more immersive and enriching experience of visualisation or other advanced practices.

The first few steps in meditation guide your brainwaves from beta to alpha, theta, and delta states mirroring wakefulness to sleep, where deep insights, creativity, intuition, and healing reside. Further steps reshape neuropsychobiology, rewiring neural pathways, awakening dormant faculties, and uncovering your extraordinary potential. So, take it step by step, and you'll find yourself reaching new heights in your meditation journey.

At times if you ever feel that the sequential suggestions are 'a-lot-to-do', let go and JUST BE! That could happen spontaneously at any time. Just let go of the following sequence then. Just be now and here, in complete stillness and bliss....you have arrived.

WHO SHOULD PRACTISE MEDITATION?

In a word: everyone. Meditation, when practised consistently, has benefits for everyone. But especially for:

1. **Leaders and executives:** You're at the helm, making decisions that impact many lives. Through meditation, you'll quickly be able to find the tranquillity within the storm, hone your

leadership skills, and make choices that echo clarity and wisdom.

2. **Athletes and sports enthusiasts:** Let meditation be your secret weapon for optimal performance, mental resilience, and laser-like focus. Through meditation, you'll flourish into the athlete who inspires, both on and off the field.

3. **Fashion influencers and industry professionals:** Your creativity, when fused with mindfulness, will expand like never before. Tap into your authentic self and watch as your creations become extensions of your spirit, capturing hearts and minds.

4. **Homemakers and stay-at-home parents**: Amidst the hustle of daily chores and caring for your loved ones, meditation provides an opportunity for self-care. Discover balance, stress relief, and nurture a harmonious living environment, transforming your home into a sanctuary of peace.

5. **Students and young minds:** Meditation will facilitate a smooth navigation of the highs and lows of growing up with grace and resilience. Make meditation your compass during these transformative years, guiding your path towards self-discovery and mental well-being.

6. **Entrepreneurs and business owners:** Entrepreneurs, it's time to unlock uncharted terrains of your mind. Meditation will supercharge your ventures with enhanced focus, creativity, and clarity to manifest success that echoes beyond balance sheets.

7. **Doctors, healthcare professionals, and caregivers:** As you optimise the wellbeing of others, meditation will offer you the chance to optimise your own. Amidst your noble and demanding profession, equip yourself with tools for personal wellness and emotional balance.

8. **Spiritual seekers:** Just watch as meditation slowly unveils the mysteries of your true self. Embark on an exhilarating journey of self-discovery, spiritual wisdom and inner transformation.

9. **Passionate individuals:** Aspiring for personal growth and self-improvement? It's meditation that will allow you to unlock your full potential.

HOW TO MEDITATE – THE BASIC PRINCIPLES

By now we have become aware that meditation encompasses relaxation, contemplation, self-reflection, healing, and personal growth. Healing involves releasing negative impressions and the emotions attached to them, while personal growth is the transformative process of deep introspection and discovering our true abilities—a self that seeks love, joy, and abundance. While the book's "Must-Do" section provides a step-by-step approach, let's explore the basic principles for an immersive meditative experience.

First, you would create a peaceful and quiet space where you can sit or lie down comfortably without distractions. You would adopt a relaxed yet alert posture, whether sitting cross-legged, in a chair with your feet flat on the ground, or lying down on your back (depending on the meditation). Then you would begin focusing on your breath as mentioned before, using it to tap into a calm and peaceful state of mind. The breath would be your anchor, allowing you to stay present in the moment.

As you meditate, however, thoughts, feelings, and sensations will naturally come up. Instead of judging or getting carried away by them, that's when you would maintain a non-judgmental awareness and gently return your focus to your chosen focal point (e.g., breath) whenever distractions arise. From there, you would begin climbing the meditation ladder as described earlier.

All the while, you would remain as still as possible, with your eyes closed.

At the end of the meditation, you would slowly introduce some movement back into the body before opening your eyes and gently moving on with the rest of your day.

The 2b diagram in the illustration section of the book shows meditation ladder along with the specific actions or states that each step leads to.

KEY POINTS:

1. Our innate nature seeks joy and peace: two elements that meditation facilitates.

2. Meditation is like a ladder we must climb, from basic to advanced. All meditations have the same foundation, but have very different results.

3. Meditation has been found to enhance our physical, mental and spiritual well being, laying the foundation for a healthy and fulfilled life. It heals, transforms and helps create a reality we desire.

SOUL WORK:

1. **Reflect on your productive beliefs** - those beliefs that empower and support your growth, well-being, and success. For example, 'I believe that I can achieve anything I set my mind to.'

2. **Identify your non-productive beliefs** - beliefs that hinder or limit your potential, self-worth, or ability to achieve your goals. For example, 'I don't make friends easily.'

3. **Consider three new beliefs you would like to adopt** - beliefs that will empower you, enhance your self-confidence, and help you manifest your desires. For example: 'I'm an interesting person who is able to nurture new friendships,' 'I'm

worthy of receiving a high wage,' and 'My meditation journey is taking me to new heights in my personal growth.'

Chapter 3

The Badass Meditator – A Fusion of Ancient Wisdom and Modern Science

"Science is not only compatible with spirituality; it is a profound source of spirituality."

- Carl Sagan

The term "badass" in the context of meditation represents a dynamic fusion of science and spirituality, blending traditional wisdom with scientific understanding. This approach acknowledges the rich heritage of traditional meditation practices while embracing the insights and advancements of modern science. The term "badass meditator" represents a fearless and empowered approach to meditation that embraces individuality and authenticity.

This concept involves going beyond the stereotype of meditation as just a relaxation technique or simply "sitting in silence." Instead, it's about being able to use the practice as a means of making real change in your life through commitment, dedication, and daily inspired action to cultivate a deep level of mindfulness, concentration, and insight.

To be a badass meditator means embodying certain qualities and principles:

1. **Fearless Commitment:** A badass meditator is dedicated and unwavering in their commitment to the practice. They embrace challenges and obstacles, recognising that true growth occurs when stepping outside their comfort zones.

2. **Authentic Self-Expression:** A badass meditator honours their unique journey and experiences. They understand that meditation is not about

conforming to a specific mould but about embracing and expressing their individuality authentically.

3. **Inner Strength and Resilience:** Being a badass meditator involves cultivating inner strength and resilience. They stay centred and grounded amidst adversity and turbulent emotions, using meditation as a tool for emotional healing and personal transformation. They fearlessly push boundaries, challenge limitations, and bring the principles of mindfulness, compassion, and self-awareness to their interactions and decisions to co-create a new reality. By doing so, they extend their practice beyond formal sessions, inspire others, and create a ripple effect of positive change in their immediate environment and beyond.

4. **Unleashing Potential:** A badass meditator recognizes and taps into their full potential. They explore deeper states of consciousness, heightened awareness, and profound insights. Meditation becomes a catalyst for self-discovery, wisdom, and personal growth.

5. **Empowered Creation:** A badass meditator understands their power to create their reality, not just be a victim of it. They align their intentions with their actions, manifesting positive

change in their own lives and making a meaningful impact in the world.

Diagram 3a in the illustration section of the book shows the qualities of a badass meditator.

The fusion of ancient meditation practice and modern science is nothing but fusion of experience and knowledge. Experience without knowledge is chaos and knowledge without experience is a dusted library. Experience and knowledge together is transformation.

KEY POINTS:

1. A badass meditator represents the fusion of science and spirituality.
2. Consistent practice, trust, and commitment are key factors for a dedicated meditator.

SOUL WORK:

1. Make a fearless commitment to your meditation practice.
2. Start expressing your authentic self.
3. Embrace change and trust your intuition.
4. Engage in self-reflection on a regular basis.
5. Trust in your inner power for personal growth and transformation.

Chapter 4

Overcoming the Big 5 Obstacles

"Only in my pain, did I find my will,

Only in my chaos, did I learn to be still,

Only in my fear, did I find my might.

Only in my darkness, did I see my light."

- T.M.T.

To say that meditation is easy is erroneous. It's a journey, one that begins with removing what's holding you back from taking the first step. There may be doubts and misconceptions surrounding meditation which can hinder people from meditating in the first place, as well as practical blockers, all of which we will explore in this chapter. But by overcoming these hurdles, you'll emerge as a true badass meditator - resilient, empowered, and centred. It's time to turn your challenges into victories.

After conducting a survey of the most common obstacles, here are the top five that we'll explore in this chapter:

1. **A misguided belief system:** Many people believe that meditation is only for spiritual or religious individuals. Some individuals wonder why they should meditate if they're not overtly suffering and feel fine on a day-to-day basis. Others believe that it plainly doesn't work, and if it does work, it's merely a form of escapism that has no real, long-lasting effects. No matter what our beliefs may be, they completely dictate our experiences and our results. Therefore, it's vital (if we want true success in anything we do, including meditation) that our beliefs support what we actually want to accomplish.

2. **Time constraints:** Many individuals feel they don't have enough time to meditate, especially those who juggle various priorities. However, meditation offers more than just a temporary escape or relief from stress and is well worth the investment. It provides an opportunity for self-reflection, inner growth, and cultivating a sense of presence and peace in daily life, therefore supercharging your productivity and motivation. It has a great influence on people around you too. So even if it's just 10 minutes per day, meditation should be considered just as much of a priority as your daily shower.

3. **A mind that's 'too busy' for meditation:** I've heard countless people report that meditation isn't for them because their minds wander off too easily. While it's true that a person with intrusive thoughts and emotions may struggle with meditation at first, it's actually this type of person that needs meditation the most. And nobody, I repeat, nobody, has a mind that is inappropriate for meditation. The busier your mind is, the more you need it.

4. **Lack of technique and boredom:** Many individuals struggle to maintain a consistent meditation ritual due to a lack of proper training and support, which is pivotal to building a successful practice. Within this chaos, boredom is

more likely to strike, putting people off the idea entirely. With a solid framework, however, meditation is a never-ending, ever-changing journey, and is anything but boring!

5. **An inability to integrate the benefits in real-world scenarios:** For many, the world resumes its chaotic dance quickly after meditation. And if they only observe its effects for the time they're sitting, meditation will travel to the bottom of their to-do lists very quickly. Integrating its magic off the meditation cushion and into daily life is an art, one you'll learn in this book. This in and of itself is incredibly motivating, as a short investment of time per day brings major shifts and results in real life.

Now let's dive into each obstacle in more detail in order to open the door to the magic of meditation, starting with number 1: a misguided belief system.

REWIRING A MISGUIDED BELIEF SYSTEM

Our belief systems greatly influence how we perceive reality, but they are not absolute truths. These beliefs are deeply ingrained in us from childhood and are influenced by various external factors such as culture, education, and media. However, to adapt to an ever-evolving world, it is important to challenge and examine our belief systems to bring about meaningful change in our lives.

One area where this is particularly relevant is in the understanding and practice of meditation. Meditation has often been misunderstood and associated with vague concepts, leading to misconceptions and scepticism. Many people believe it is only for spiritual or religious individuals, or that it is a form of escapism. Some even dismiss it as a passing fad or question its real benefits. These beliefs stem from what we have been told, what we see around us, and our cultural backgrounds. To name a few, meditation has been proven to be highly effective when it comes to:

Reducing stress and anxiety: One of the most well-known benefits of meditation is its ability to reduce stress and anxiety. Regular meditation practice helps activate the body's relaxation response, leading to a decrease in stress hormones like cortisol. Regular meditation practice brings changes in the brain, including increased activity in areas associated with emotional regulation and decreased activity in areas associated with stress and anxiety. As a result, we often experience a sense of calm and inner peace. Numerous randomised controlled trials have shown that meditation leads to a significant increase in feelings of emotional wellbeing.

Improving focus and concentration: Meditation is like a workout for the mind, strengthening our ability to focus and sustain attention. This heightened focus can lead to improved productivity and efficiency in daily tasks. Meditation training can enhance working memory capacity, a key component of cognitive functioning.

Enhancing self-awareness: Meditation encourages self-reflection and introspection. By observing thoughts and emotions without judgement, individuals gain insights into their inner world. Meditation fosters greater self-awareness, self-esteem, and self-acceptance. This enhanced self-awareness can lead to a deeper understanding of behavioural patterns and emotional reactions, allowing room for change and growth.

Improving sleep: Meditation improves sleep quality and reduces insomnia by calming the mind and reducing activation of the sympathetic nervous system responsible for the fight-or-flight response. Many people struggle with sleep issues due to racing thoughts and restlessness. Meditation promotes relaxation and a sense of tranquillity, making it easier to fall asleep and achieve deeper slumber. By calming the mind, meditation can also help reduce the occurrence of insomnia.

Boosting overall well-being: Meditation significantly improves overall well-being, including reducing symptoms of depression and anxiety, enhancing positive emotions, and increasing life satisfaction, as evidenced by systematic reviews of randomised controlled trials. A regular practice cultivates emotional resilience, enabling individuals to better navigate life's challenges.

Enhancing physical health: Beyond its mental and emotional benefits, meditation positively influences physical health. It has been linked to reduced blood pressure, improved heart health, and boosted immune function.

Promoting the mind-body connection: Meditation helps strengthen the connection between the mind and body. By being attuned to bodily sensations and breath, we become more aware of our physical state. This heightened mind-body connection can lead to better self-care and a more profound appreciation of the body's signals.

Managing chronic pain: For individuals suffering from chronic pain conditions, meditation can be a valuable tool for pain management. By redirecting focus and developing a non-reactive attitude towards pain, meditation can reduce the perception of pain and improve overall quality of life.

Fostering empathy and compassion: Loving-kindness meditation, a type of meditation that involves generating feelings of compassion and empathy, has been shown to increase feelings of empathy and promote prosocial behaviour. It enhances our ability to connect with others and cultivate harmonious relationships.

Strengthening resilience: Life is filled with ups and downs, and meditation equips individuals with the tools to cope with adversity. By developing resilience through meditation, people can bounce back more easily from setbacks and challenges. This has also been proven in legitimate studies on those facing major life changes.

Promoting positive behaviours: Regular meditation has been associated with a reduction in impulsive and addictive behaviours. It helps individuals become more aware of their habits and reactions, making it easier to break free from harmful patterns.

As you can see, the field of meditation has experienced exponential growth in research and evidence in recent years. Scientific studies have demonstrated the profound effects of meditation on our entire system. My intention behind sharing this with you is to help dispel your misconceptions and shed light on the true potential of meditation as a transformative practice.

Meditation serves as a bridge between modern science, spirituality, and human potential. By engaging in deep introspection and self-examination during meditation, we can cleanse our thoughts and emotions, leading to healing on physical, mental, and spiritual levels. It helps us become more present and aware, bringing clarity to our minds, improving decision-making, and enhancing our overall effectiveness.

Furthermore, most of the world's top achievers have integrated meditation as part of their lives. Some notable examples include Oprah Winfrey: the much-loved media mogul and philanthropist who has been a keen transcendental meditator for over 30 years. Then there's Ray Dalio: the billionaire investor and founder of Bridgewater Associates, who attributes much of his success to his daily meditation practice. There's Arianna Huffington, the co-founder of The Huffington Post, LeBron James, the NBA superstar who credited visualisation meditation as a key component of his mental training and performance on the basketball court, Jeff Weiner, the former CEO of LinkedIn who advocates for mindfulness practices, ...the list goes on and on and on. These individuals recognize the benefits of meditation in promoting mental clarity, reducing stress, and enhancing overall well-being, which in turn contributes to their achievements in various fields.

To empower ourselves fully, we must go beyond surface-level negative beliefs and question their origins. Our beliefs like the classic "I'm not good enough" are shaped by external influences, but they are not absolute truths. We have the power to rewire our belief system, freeing ourselves from doubts and limitations. We don't even have to wait for science or other people to validate our beliefs or experiences. The frontiers of knowledge are ever-expanding, and what may seem unconventional today could become widely accepted in the future.

In the modern world, we often carry the weight of past impressions and face the demands of a fast-paced society. External stimuli, along with our past experiences and beliefs, can influence our self-image, self-esteem, and self-confidence, giving rise to negative emotions. This inner conflict between our thoughts and emotions disrupts the coherence within ourselves, leading us to wear masks that cover our true selves, and the people we actually want to be. This lack of coherence affects our clarity of mind, self-awareness, and decision-making abilities, making us ineffective and dissatisfied with our results.

To maintain the coherence of our head and heart, it is crucial to address these negative emotions. Engaging in practices that induce powerful states and positive emotions can help us maintain sanity, clarity, efficiency, decisiveness, and effectiveness. We don't need to put off self-exploration for a crisis, loss, trauma, tragedy, or disease to prompt us to examine who we are, what we are doing, how we are living, and what we believe. Through deep introspection during meditation, we can cleanse our thoughts and emotions on a deep level, benefiting us physically, mentally, and spiritually.

Healing the pain of our past, and therefore our negative belief systems, we give ourselves the opportunity to be born anew, bringing more coherence, synchronicities, smoother experiences, better relationships, and improved health. This is why we meditate.

Ultimately, the responsibility for our own transformation lies within us, and through meditation, we embark on the noble path of true self-empowerment and personal development.

LOOSENING TIME CONSTRAINTS

Now we're feeling more positive about meditation in general, having addressed our negative belief systems in the name of replacing them with empowering ones, we're ready to tackle the second obstacle; that of time.

There's a classic Zen proverb that states:

"You should sit in meditation for twenty minutes every day — unless you're too busy. Then you should sit for an hour."

It's a paradox, but nevertheless, it has a lot of truth to it. The busier and more stressed you are, the more you actually need meditation. Having no time is a common obstacle to meditation, but it is one that can be overcome with commitment, discipline, and a genuine desire to transform. While it may seem challenging to find time, incorporating meditation into your daily routine can actually increase your efficiency and productivity, ultimately creating more time for you in the long run. By investing a small amount of time in meditation, you can reap significant rewards in terms of mental clarity and time management.

James Clear, the author of "Atomic Habits," emphasises the power of small habits in creating long-term change. Making incremental improvements of just one percent each day may not seem notable at the moment, but over time, the cumulative impact is enormous. The same principle applies to meditation.

By consciously allocating some time for meditation, you can create a habit that yields tremendous benefits. As I mentioned before, if we have time for a ten-minute shower per day, we also have time for a ten-minute meditation. A fool-proof way of doing this is by simply setting our alarm clocks to go off ten minutes earlier. If you're resistant to losing out on ten minutes in bed, you can always block out another dedicated time in your schedule, or stack the meditation habit on top of existing routines, injecting mindfulness into your breakfast, lunch and dinner.

Many people often wonder how I manage to find time for meditation, painting, writing, and working full-time while taking care of my two children. When I first began meditating, my meditation practice was irregular, and I often struggled with doubt and procrastination, which still occurs at times. It took going through personal crises to truly recognize the value of meditation and start using my time consciously.

As I committed to a regular meditation practice, I noticed a significant improvement in my focus and productivity.

I found that I could complete my work in half the time I used to take, allowing me to create space for more deep work and self-expression. Meditation became a catalyst that introduced me to my passion. What began as curiosity merged with desperation transformed into a deep sense of purpose and a complete transformation of my body, mind, and soul.

And it isn't just me. Some of the busiest people out there always make time for meditation, because they're aware of its countless benefits. With meditation, you really do get more out than you put in. Finding time for what truly matters requires taking action and making conscious choices. It is through these deliberate efforts we can create a fulfilling and balanced life.

To create time for meditation, make it a priority and schedule it into your calendar. Start with small increments and gradually increase the duration if you can. Find a consistent time and create a designated meditation space to cultivate a habit. If you have children, rely on your partner to take over for the duration of your meditation, or offer them a gold sticker for giving you 'quiet' time. Incorporate meditation into your daily routine and consider using guided meditations or apps for support.

When looking at your calendar, odds are you're spending some part of the day doing things you a) don't need to do and b) aren't important. So consider swapping some unproductive habits, for example, your social media scrolling time, for meditation.

Additionally, I recommend sharing your intention to incorporate meditation into your routine with a trusted friend or family member. Ask them to hold you accountable. If that's not available to you, consider joining meditation groups or online communities for additional motivation and guidance.

EMBRACING YOUR 'TOO BUSY' MIND

Once you've integrated your positive beliefs about meditation, as well as having carved out some time to practise, it's time to turn inwards.

For those who struggle with an overactive mind, this is for you. And big news–you're not alone. Many of us don't realise that, despite how uncomfortable meditation may feel at first, we're not especially inept. Every single person on planet Earth who started to meditate surely felt overwhelmed at first.

Steve Jobs, Co-founder of Apple Inc., had this to say: *"If you just sit and observe, you will see how restless your mind is. If you try to calm it, it only makes things worse, but over time it does calm, and when it does, there's room to hear more subtle things - that's when your intuition starts to blossom and you start to see things more clearly and be in the present more. Your mind just slows down, and you see a tremendous expanse in the moment. You see so much more than you could see before."*

Our thoughts are an inherent part of our being, and it's important to acknowledge their power and influence. On a daily basis, research suggests that the average person has approximately 60,000 to 80,000 thoughts. While some thoughts pass by without evoking any emotions, repetitive and connected thoughts can lead to stress and negative emotions.

The key lies in understanding that thoughts, in themselves, have no inherent power and that they're absolutely normal. Just as our heart beats, our mind thinks. That said, we can choose to not place so much importance on them. When we engage with specific thoughts, it triggers corresponding emotions, leading to a shift in our emotional state and influencing our actions. That's what makes thoughts feel significant. This negative spiral of thoughts and emotions can have physical manifestations, such as headaches, fatigue, unhappiness, and sadness, therefore, many people avoid meditation, believing that meditation caused these states of being.

However, we have the ability to overpower thoughts that don't serve us, and nourish those that do. Research supports the practice of meditation and conscious breathing as effective tools for managing and redirecting our thoughts. By actively focusing on the breath and allowing thoughts to come and go without getting entangled in them, we can interrupt the negative thought patterns and promote a sense of calm and wellbeing. It is an art that can be learned, and the breath becomes our secret weapon in this process. Slow the breath, slow the mind.

Apart from breathing deeply as a way to slow down the mind, we can also take action before our meditation practice, releasing some restless energy through short bursts of rapid physical activity, such as shaking and jumping up and down on the spot. You may also choose to have a short Journaling session, known as 'brain dump Journaling,' to get your thoughts out on paper so they don't take too much of your attention as you meditate.

However busy your mind is, just remember that meditation will bring nothing but benefits and that over time, you WILL see progress, and your mind will eventually get clearer.

LACK OF TECHNIQUE AND BOREDOM

A lack of technique in meditation can be a significant barrier that prevents people from fully engaging in the practice. Meditation, like any skill, requires guidance and understanding of the proper techniques to be effective. Without proper instruction or knowledge of different meditation methods, individuals may struggle to find their focus, experience frustration, and eventually give up on the practice altogether.

Beginners often struggle with improper posture, for example, leading to physical discomfort and making it difficult to relax and concentrate. Similarly, improper breathing techniques can disrupt the flow of meditation and prevent individuals from reaching a deeper state of relaxation. Additionally, without guidance on how to handle certain experiences during meditation, such as emotional releases or encountering challenging thoughts, individuals may feel overwhelmed or unsure of how to proceed. Combine that without a well-executed time slot, and without any practical audio guidance, you also have a recipe for boredom.

You will learn exactly how to deal with these situations in the later chapters of this book.

Preparation is the antidote to failure.

To overcome these obstacles, it is crucial to seek proper guidance and education on meditation techniques. Attending meditation classes, using guided meditation apps, or reading books on meditation can provide valuable insights and techniques to enhance the meditative experience. Learning how to work with thoughts, emotions, and bodily sensations during meditation can help individuals navigate through potential barriers and develop a fulfilling meditation practice. With patience, perseverance, and the right techniques, individuals can overcome the hurdles and reap the numerous benefits that meditation offers for mental, emotional, and physical wellbeing.

AN INABILITY TO INTEGRATE THE BENEFITS IN REAL-WORLD SCENARIOS

As we now know, meditation is a powerful practice that has been proven to bring numerous physical, mental, and emotional benefits. It helps reduce stress, improve focus, enhance emotional well-being, and promote overall inner peace. However, despite its numerous advantages, many people find it challenging to integrate the benefits of meditation into their daily lives beyond the meditation cushion.

One of the main reasons for this difficulty is the stark contrast between the meditative state and the fast-paced, demanding nature of modern life. On the meditation cushion, individuals can find a tranquil space to connect with their inner selves, but as soon as they step off, they are thrust back into the hustle and bustle of everyday life. The serene state cultivated during meditation can quickly dissipate, leaving individuals struggling to maintain that sense of calm in the face of various stressors and distractions.

Additionally, meditation often requires consistency and patience to see long-term benefits, as discussed. Many people approach meditation with high expectations, hoping for immediate results in their 'outer worlds,' aka, their relationships, their productivity, their manifestation skills and all-round general health. Without immediate gratification, individuals may feel discouraged and abandon the practice altogether, missing out on its potential benefits.

To overcome these challenges, it's essential to approach meditation with a realistic mindset and an understanding of its transformative potential over time. Incorporating shorter meditation sessions throughout the day can also help maintain mindfulness and awareness in the midst of busyness. Furthermore, practising self-compassion and letting go of rigid expectations can enable individuals to embrace the meditation journey without feeling discouraged by perceived shortcomings. The change will come, little by little, day by day. And it's well worth your perseverance.

KEY POINTS:

1. **Let go of preconceived notions:** Often, our beliefs about meditation are influenced by preconceived notions we may have from media or cultural stereotypes. Try to let go of these preconceived notions and approach meditation with an open mind.

2. **Make time for what matters most**: Recognize that self-care, including meditation, is crucial for your overall well-being. Make it a priority by scheduling dedicated time for yourself each day, even if it's just a few minutes. Treat it as an essential part of your routine, like eating or sleeping.

3. **Know that busy minds are perfectly suited to meditation:** Just because you have a mind filled with thoughts and emotions, doesn't mean that meditation isn't for you!

4. **The benefits of meditation will manifest in your real life:** Be patient. You'll begin to see the huge benefits of meditation slowly, and over time with consistent practice.

SOUL WORK:

1. Make a list of any negative beliefs you have about meditation and replace them with positive ones. E.g. 'Meditation isn't for me,' to 'I'm perfect for meditation!'

2. Choose a 10-minute slot in your calendar for meditation every single day. From there, you can lengthen the time if you choose. I recommend first thing in the morning.

3. If you have a very busy mind while meditating, observe which thoughts tend to repeat themselves. From there, perhaps you can begin to solve these issues so they don't interrupt you so much. E.g. If you keep thinking about what you'll cook for dinner, make a meal plan at the beginning of the week so you don't have to think about it!

4. Make a commitment to learning different meditation techniques from professionals to support you in your meditation journey (you've already started by reading this book!)

5. Be mindful of the subtle changes you begin to see in your mental health and in your

relationships as you leave the meditation cushion.

Chapter 5

The 'Must-Know' of Meditation

"The body achieves what the mind believes."

- Napoleon Hill

Over my years of practice, my understanding of meditation has blossomed, allowing me to tap into its transformative power. Meditation is a tapestry woven with threads of ancient wisdom, scientific discoveries, spiritual insights, and metaphysical and psychological frameworks.

Meditation invites us to explore the profound interconnectedness of the mind, brain, and body, highlighting that our thoughts and emotions directly influence the structure and function of our brain, which in turn affects our physical and mental well-being. By paying attention to our thoughts and intentionally directing them in a positive and constructive way, we tangibly transform the brain's wiring. It's been scientifically proven that we can influence the physical brain structure and its functions. This infinitely enhances various cognitive abilities and, of course, our mental and emotional well-being.

Metaphysically, meditation brings us a deep understanding of the relationship between mind, brain and body, and the expansive nature of human consciousness. It also allows us to explore concepts like higher states of awareness and the interconnectedness of all things.

Spiritually, meditation is a means to deepen the connection with the divine, whatever we deem that to be, as well as providing a sturdy foundation for inner wisdom, compassion and love.

Psychologically, it is a tool for stress reduction, emotional regulation, and personal growth, which is why the NHS is now incorporating it into therapeutic approaches to healing.

The mind, brain and body are intricately connected. *Where the mind goes, the brain and body follows. An unmanaged mind means an unmanaged brain, and an unmanaged brain means an unmanaged body and consequently, an unmanaged life. It is a two-way street, and the reverse is also true. The way we live life influences our bodies, brains and minds,* says Dr Caroline Leaf, clinical and cognitive neuroscientist.

An example is, drama at work can activate the body's stress response, leading to increased heart rate, elevated blood pressure, and compromised immune function. On the other hand, a visit to the spa or a soothing meditation session brings about a calm state of mind which promotes relaxation, improves immune function, and supports overall well-being. Conversely, our physical health can also affect our mental and emotional states. Chronic pain, illness, or imbalances in the body can contribute to feelings of stress, depression, or anxiety. It's all linked. Diagram 5a in the illustrations section of the book shows the connection between the mind, brain and body.

THE MIND VS THE BRAIN

We will kickstart this chapter by first describing the difference between the mind and the brain. This is crucial in order to understand exactly what meditation does. Contrary to popular belief, the mind and brain are two related but distinct concepts. The mind drives the brain. The brain is a physical organ, and communicates with the rest of the body through a complex network of neurons, neuropeptides, neurotransmitters, and hormones, relaying signals and facilitating various bodily functions. It is a responder and reactor.

The mind filters every experience and our thoughts and feelings about them, into the brain, and it responds on an electromagnetic, electrochemical, quantum and genetic level. The genetic response changes the physical structure of the brain (neuroplasticity). Therefore, the brain uses this information provided by the mind to create a protein that holds the information in vibrations. Ever heard about the notion that certain people have positive or negative 'vibes?' I imagine that this is where the phrase came from. We can see and study the brain's 'vibes' through neuroimaging and neurophysiology.

If this is all new to you, you may still be wondering what the mind is. I'm guessing that understanding what the brain is wasn't so difficult, as it's something we can see, feel and research with relative ease. There is plenty of literature and academic papers on the subject. The mind, however, is a more abstract concept and difficult to properly study. It refers to the collection of mental processes that occur *within* the brain, including thoughts, emotions, perceptions, memories, and beliefs. Many philosophers and scientists argue that the mind is much more than just the activity of the brain, and that there may be non-physical or spiritual aspects to it. The mind, also known as our 'consciousness,' remains a mysterious concept to humanity.

The human mind is divided into the non-conscious, subconscious, and conscious.

The non-conscious mind is a state of mind that occurs outside of our awareness. It is automatic. It works day and night. It also includes repressed memories and desires, a wide range of automatic processes (examples include regulating body temperature, heart rate, and breathing), cognitive biases, as well as storing long-term memories and ingrained habits that can influence our behaviour and decision-making. No thinking is required for it to work.

The subconscious is like a bridge between the non-conscious and conscious mind. While we are not always aware of the workings of our subconscious mind, it can have a powerful impact on our thoughts, emotions, and behaviour. When we learn to pay attention to what is coming from our non-conscious mind to the subconscious mind, we can start changing our mind, which then changes our brain and body. The subconscious mind plays a vital role in shaping our beliefs, attitudes, and behaviour patterns, often influenced by past experiences and conditioning. Our memories shape our understanding of the world and ourselves and help us to navigate our lives and make decisions based on these past experiences.

The subconscious mind is also referred to as the 'emotional non analytical mind' that uses higher faculties such as imagination, will, intuition, memory, reason, and perception. The subconscious mind runs on habits and automatic programming. Emotions, the language of the subconscious, play a key role in our decision-making, social interactions, and overall well-being.

On the other hand, the conscious mind, the 'logical analytical mind' is the high level of awareness that we experience in our daily lives. Our five senses (sight, hearing, smell, touch and taste) control the conscious mind. It encompasses our overt thoughts, perceptions, reasoning, and decision-making processes. It is the part of the mind that we actively engage with and can exercise control over easily. The conscious mind allows us to observe and analyse our thoughts, make choices, and respond to the external world. It is the seat of our self-awareness and cognitive abilities.

You can thank your conscious mind for your ability to read these words and understand them. How you feel about them, however, is down to your subconscious. And the fact that you didn't forget to breathe whilst reading? That's your unconscious mind at work. The relationship between these levels of the mind is very dynamic and interconnected.

So what does all this have to do with meditation badassey?

Deep introspection in meditation helps us delve into the subconscious mind, bring unconscious patterns to light, and reshape our conscious experiences. You can regrow and change the structures of the brain and improve the health of your body and life this way. By working with the different levels of the mind, we can optimally self-regulate and self-soothe in times of adversity. We can train ourselves to manage the mind, which then manages our brain, our body health, and our life. It is a cumulative change over time. This is our motivation behind reprogramming the brain during meditation.

Meditation opens the door between the two minds we can gain mastery over; the subconscious and conscious mind. Reprogramming the subconscious mind often refers to the process of changing deeply ingrained beliefs, thoughts, and habits that are stored there. These beliefs and habits may be limiting, self-sabotaging, or harmful in some way, and can prevent individuals from reaching their full potential. Neuroscientific research has revealed that regular meditation practice can lead to changes in brain regions associated with attention, emotion regulation, and self-awareness. These changes are believed to contribute to improved cognitive functions, emotional well-being, and resilience.

From a psychological perspective, meditation can help cultivate mental well-being by reducing anxiety, depression, and rumination. Anxiety and depression are messengers from the unconscious mind (not the conscious or even the subconscious, which is why these mental illnesses feel out of our control) from adverse experiences like trauma, abuse, and loss as well as socioeconomic and socioenvironmental issues like, say, a global pandemic or climate change. The immune system works with these adverse experiences in the same way it does for pathogens, activating a CODE RED response and causing dysfunctional brain change. Anxiety and depression are the two signals of this change. We can retrace our steps and track back to our anxiety/despression's origin during meditation, as well as dismantle our negative beliefs that came with our trauma during meditation. By training the mind to observe thoughts, emotions and even trauma without judgement, meditation enables individuals to respond to challenges with greater self-compassion, clarity and equanimity.

As well as healing deep psychological wounds, reprogramming the subconscious mind in meditative states can be a powerful tool for personal growth and transformation. That's to say, we can take our lives from good to great by overcoming limiting beliefs and behaviours, in order to reach our full potential.

There are several techniques that can be used to reprogram the subconscious mind, including:

1. **Affirmations:** Affirmations are positive statements that are repeated regularly in order to change negative thought patterns and beliefs. By repeating positive affirmations, individuals can gradually replace negative self-talk with more positive and empowering beliefs. For example, changing, 'I'm not good enough to attract a partner,' to 'I'm worthy of love,' or quite simply 'I can't do this,' to 'I can do this.'

2. **Visualisation:** Visualisation involves creating mental images of positive outcomes or experiences. By visualising success and positive outcomes, individuals can program their subconscious mind to focus on positive outcomes rather than negative ones.

3. **Hypnosis:** Hypnosis is a technique that involves inducing a trance-like state in order to access the subconscious mind. During hypnosis, individuals can work with a therapist or hypnotist to identify and change negative thought patterns, behaviours and beliefs.

4. **Meditation:** Meditation quiets the mind and focuses on the present moment. By practising meditation regularly, we can increase awareness of our thoughts and feelings and learn to observe and change negative thought patterns even off the meditation cushion.

5. **Repetition:** Repetition is a simple but effective technique for reprogramming the subconscious mind. By repeating positive affirmations, using positive language or focusing on positive thoughts and feelings, individuals can gradually shift their subconscious mind towards a happier, more empowering state of being.

So as you can see, in the words of Matthieu Ricard, "Meditation is not just blissing out under a tree. It completely changes your brain and therefore changes what you are."

It's incredible how these techniques reprogram the subconscious by rewiring the brain and altering its internal chemical balance. This process involves changing deeply ingrained thought patterns and beliefs, which can lead to shifts in neural connections and neurotransmitter activity. By consciously choosing to think and act in new ways, individuals can create new neural pathways, reinforcing desired behaviours and attitudes. This rewiring can also influence the brain's chemistry, affecting emotions, reactions, and overall well-being. It's a profound demonstration of the brain's plasticity and the power of the mind to shape our reality.

MEDITATION, NEURO-ELECTRICITY AND BRAINWAVES

Neuro-electricity refers to the electrical and electromagnetic activity generated by the brain. Thoughts born in the conscious mind have energy and operate on frequencies, or 'vibes.' When they are fed into the brain, nerve cells (neurons) fire and exchange charge elements. This creates an electromagnetic field vibrating at various frequencies generating four types of brain waves: beta, alpha, theta and delta waves. These brain waves are detected using sensors placed on the scalp called electroencephalograms. Each wave corresponds to a different state of mind, from deep sleep to wakefulness and focused attention. Diagram 5b in the illustration section of the book shows the brain waves and related state of being.

Meditation has a profound influence on brainwave patterns, allowing individuals to access altered states of consciousness. Understanding these brainwave states is essential as we advance in our meditation journey.

A breakdown of the brainwaves:

Beta waves: When the brain is aroused and actively engaged in mental activities, it generates beta waves.

These beta waves are of relatively low amplitude and are the fastest of the four different brainwaves. The frequency of beta waves ranges from 15 to 40 cycles a second. Beta waves are characteristics of a strongly engaged mind. A person in active conversation would be in beta. A debater would be in high beta. A person making a speech, a teacher or a talk show host would all be in beta when they are engaged in their work. Low-range beta states are relaxed and interesting, for example, book reading at 13-15 Hertz. Mid-range Beta involves focused attention and learning at 16-22 Hertz. High range beta is 22-50 hz and occurs in stressful situations and high arousal states. In this high beta state, we cannot learn, heal, and behave in optimal, calm, collected ways, as quite frankly, we're freaking out! High beta waves are a result of anxiety, worry, anger, fear, frustration, and uncertainty. It knocks us out of balance and can be chronic and uncontrolled. It's the ultimate unhealthy cocktail of brain stress chemicals and an unbalanced nervous system. Living in such states affects the heart, digestion, immune function, and nervous system. If stuck in this state, one overreacts, reasons poorly, is blocked creatively and is fixated only on survival. This is the state when we're most selfish and difficult to be around.

Deep breathing and relaxing physically and mentally during the initial stages of meditation help calm down beta waves, reducing stress and promoting relaxation, creativity, and productivity.

Alpha waves: The next brainwave category in order of frequency is alpha. Where beta represents arousal, alpha represents non-arousal. Alpha brain waves indicate a state of relaxation and reflection. Alpha brain waves are slower, and higher in amplitude. Their frequency ranges from 9 to 14 cycles per second. A person who has completed a task and sits down to rest is often in an alpha state. A person who takes time out to reflect or meditate is usually in an alpha state. A person who takes a break from a busy household and walks slowly in the garden to admire the flowers is often in an alpha state. In alpha states, we can absorb new information with ease, and we are significantly more creative. It is a wakeful relaxation, one we should aspire to be in for at least part of our day.

Deep breathing and relaxing physically and mentally during the initial stages of meditation help induce alpha states, allowing individuals to absorb new information effortlessly and tap into their creativity.

Theta waves: The next state, theta brainwaves, are typically of even greater amplitude and slower frequency. This frequency range is normally between 5 and 8 cycles a second. These waves represent daydreaming and deep relaxation. A person who has taken time off from a task and begins to daydream is often in a theta brainwave state. A person who is driving on a highway or motorway and discovers that they can't recall the last five miles is often in a theta state induced by the process of driving. Individuals who do a lot of motorway driving often get good ideas during those periods when they are in theta. Individuals who run outdoors often are in a state of mental relaxation that is slower than alpha and when in theta, they are prone to a flow of ideas. This can also occur in the shower or tub or even while shaving or brushing your hair. It is a state where tasks become so automatic that you can mentally disengage from them. The ideation that can take place during the theta state is often free flow and occurs without censorship or guilt. It is typically a very positive mental state. You also experience theta while you're just on the edge of falling asleep.

Relaxing further and going into deeper states of mind during meditation allows us to enter theta states, which foster a flow of ideas, creativity, and access to the subconscious mind.

Delta waves: The final brainwave state is delta. Here the brainwaves are of the greatest amplitude and slowest frequency. They typically centre around a range of 1.5 to 4 cycles per second. They never go down to zero because that would mean that you were brain-dead! But deep, dreamless sleep would take you down to this lowest frequency; typically, 2 to 3 cycles a second. They are prominent during deep sleep and dreamless states. While not commonly accessed during meditation, delta waves are essential for restful sleep and rejuvenation.

When we go to bed and read for a few minutes before attempting to sleep, we are likely to be in low beta. When we put the book down, turn off the lights and close our eyes, our brainwaves will descend from beta, to alpha, to theta and finally, when we fall asleep, to delta.

It is a well-known fact that humans dream in 90-minute cycles. When the delta brainwave frequencies increase into the frequency of theta brainwaves, active dreaming takes place and often becomes more experiential to the person. Typically, when this occurs there is rapid eye movement, which is characteristic of active dreaming. This is called REM and is a well-known phenomenon. When an individual awakes from a deep sleep, in preparation for getting up, their brainwave frequencies will increase through the different specific stages of brainwave activity. That is, they will increase from delta to theta and then to alpha and finally, when the alarm goes off, into beta. If that individual hits the snooze alarm button they will drop in frequency to a non-aroused state, or even into theta, or sometimes fall back to sleep in delta.

During this awakening cycle, it is possible for individuals to stay in the theta state for an extended period of say, five to 15 minutes which would allow them to have a free flow of ideas about yesterday's events or to contemplate the activities of the forthcoming day. This time can be extremely productive and can be a period of very meaningful and creative mental activity. This state is a fertile ground for true change.

Research has shown that although one brainwave state may predominate at any given time, depending on the activity level of the individual, the remaining three brain states are always present and accessible to tap into with the right training.

It's also worth mentioning that there are also very rare brain waves known as 'gamma waves' which reflect a supra-conscious state at 30 cycles per second. This is the state of enlightenment.

Meditation has been extensively studied for its effects on brainwave patterns. Various studies have found that meditation can help shift brainwaves to slower, more creative states like alpha and theta. For instance, mindfulness meditation has been shown to increase alpha brainwave activity, promoting relaxation and reducing stress. Transcendental Meditation has been associated with increased theta wave activity, fostering a flow of ideas and creativity.

Brain imaging studies have demonstrated increased connectivity and synchronisation between brain regions during meditation. These changes are linked to improved attention, emotional regulation, and cognitive performance.

By understanding our brainwaves, we can also gain insight into what time of the day we should meditate. It is more optimal and easier to meditate when we first wake up (as we've moved from delta to theta to alpha to beta) or when we're just about to go to sleep (as we're slipping from beta, to alpha to theta). In the middle of the day, it takes more effort to slip through the door of the conscious to the subconscious mind because by then, we're firmly in beta (total waking state, and perhaps, borderline stressed out).

Through the practice of meditation, individuals can cultivate a more harmonious relationship between their conscious and subconscious minds by actively changing their brainwave states.

Brainwave states aren't the only things that change as you meditate. Believe it or not, so do your hormones.

MEDITATION AND YOUR INTERNAL CHEMISTRY

The brain produces various chemicals, including neuropeptides, neurotransmitters, and hormones, that play crucial roles in regulating our emotions, thoughts, and bodily functions. Neuropeptides are small protein-like molecules used by neurons to communicate with each other. They influence the brain's activity, including pain perception and emotional responses.

Neurotransmitters are the brain's chemical messengers, transmitting signals between neurons. Examples include dopamine, the "feel-good" neurotransmitter associated with pleasure and reward. Serotonin is linked to well-being and happiness, it helps regulate mood. Norepinephrine is associated with stress, it can create feelings of anxiety or alertness. Research has shown that serotonin, dopamine, and gamma-aminobutyric acid (GABA), play important roles in mood regulation, attention, and overall brain function. Hormones are produced by glands in the endocrine system, they travel through the bloodstream to tissues and organs. Examples include, Oxytocin is known as the "love hormone," it promotes bonding and trust. Cortisol is known as the "stress hormone," it's released in response to fear or stress, leading to not-so-happy feelings.

These chemicals interact in complex ways to influence our mental state and physical health. Positive thoughts and experiences often trigger the release of "happy" chemicals like dopamine and serotonin, while negative thoughts and stress can lead to the release of "not-so-happy" chemicals like cortisol.

Meditation has been found to have a significant impact on **neurochemistry**, which refers to the chemical processes that occur in the brain and dictates the hormones your body produces as well as dictating neurotransmitter activity. While neurotransmitters are specific to the nervous system, hormones are a part of the endocrine system. Both, when balanced, are responsible for better overall health.

Regular meditation practice has been associated with changes in these neurotransmitter levels. One of the key neurotransmitters that is affected by meditation is serotonin, which is associated with happiness and feelings of well-being.

Meditation has also been found to decrease the levels of cortisol, a hormone that is released in response to stress. High levels of cortisol are associated with stressful states and have negative health outcomes such as increased heart rate, erratic breathing, restlessness, an inability to think clearly, anxiety, depression, and decreased immune function. By reducing cortisol levels, meditation helps to reduce stress and improve overall health.

You'll be able to feel all of this once you start a regular meditation practice. Something that's not so obvious to you tangibly, is how meditation plays with your neuroplasticity. I mentioned this word earlier. This is your brain's ability to adapt, slowly change and rewire in response to experiences and training. One way that meditation affects neuroplasticity is by increasing the thickness of the cortex, which is the outer layer of the brain that is responsible for many higher cognitive functions. Studies have found that regular meditation practice can lead to an increase in cortical thickness, particularly in regions of the brain involved in attention, emotional regulation, and self-awareness.

Another intangible, but very real effect of meditation is how it increases the connectivity between different regions of the brain. The brain is organised into different networks, each of which is responsible for a different function. Regular meditation practices have been found to increase the connectivity between these networks, allowing for better communication and integration between different regions of the brain allowing for advanced sensory processing, enhanced social skills and all-around improved cognitive functioning.

MEDITATION AND EPIGENETICS

Then there's **epigenetics**. Here's where your individual meditation starts to affect your children! For those of you who are new to the term, epigenetics is a field of study that explores how certain changes in gene expression can be inherited or influenced by factors other than the underlying DNA sequence itself. These changes can occur due to external environmental factors, lifestyle choices, or even intense life experiences. Epigenetic modifications do not alter the DNA sequence, but they can impact how genes are "read" and expressed, potentially leading to different outcomes in cellular function and health.

Epigenetics, in conjunction with meditation, unveils a fascinating connection between our thoughts, emotions, and the regulation of gene expression. This emerging field explores how the practice of meditation can influence the epigenetic landscape, impacting our health and wellbeing.

Chronic stress has been associated with negative impacts on health and can influence epigenetic modifications, therefore the other side of the coin, such as the peace and mental clarity that comes with meditation, can have a positive influence on epigenetic modifications. Through mechanisms not yet fully understood, the reduction in stress levels during meditation may lead to changes in the epigenetic markers attached to specific genes. This affects various biological processes, including those related to immune function, inflammation, and cellular health. This modified gene expression pattern may contribute to improved physiological responses, including enhanced resilience to stress. What a gift to give to our children!

MEDITATION AND QUANTUM PHYSICS

Finally, there's the **observer effect** and **quantum entanglement** to mention. We're about to go deep! Ready? Researchers now also believe that meditation can impact the brain at a quantum level, influencing the behaviour of subatomic particles like protons, photons, and electrons. These particles can act in strange ways at this tiny level. These particles can be in multiple places at once or switch between waves of energy and particles of matter. It's like magic happening on a very tiny scale! They have limitless probabilities, and their behaviour is not predictable until we observe it. Therefore, through the observer effect, that it, with mindful attention energy becomes matter. Therefore, with meditation, our thoughts can become our physical reality.

Quantum particles exist everywhere, connecting everything at a quantum level. This interconnectedness allows for instantaneous information sharing across any distance through quantum entanglement; the state of one particle can affect the state of another particle, even if they are physically separated. During meditation, individuals focus on the present moment and aim to connect with the universal energy through visualisations to attract their desires. Essentially, meditation taps into quantum processes in the brain and accesses the universal consciousness that extends beyond the individual.

If this last claim was hard to get your head around, or didn't resonate with you, don't worry. It's an emerging science that is attempting to explain a deeply spiritual concept: that of oneness and manifestation through meditation.

The Bhagavad Gita, a sacred Hindu scripture and one of the most important texts in Indian philosophy and spirituality, states that *"through meditation, the higher self is experienced."* The higher self is in this context being...everything.

And when you look at it, everything is energy.

It was the world-celebrated scientist Albert Einstein that said it best. "Everything is energy and that's all there is to it. Match the frequency of the reality you want and you cannot help but get that reality. It can be no other way. This is not philosophy. This is physics."

All physical things including human beings are made of matter which is made of atoms. Atoms are the building blocks of matter, composed of protons, neutrons, and electrons. Imagine the atoms as little spinning tops. They move, vibrate and have frequencies, almost like engaging in a dance. This dance of energy is happening all the time, even though we can't see it with our eyes. Scientists who study these tiny particles call this world the "quantum world." Therefore, at the subatomic level, everything is made of energy. Some people call this energy "God" while others call it "Intelligence" or "Life force" or "Spirit" or "Consciousness."

We therefore live in a quantum world, where things are not as simple as they seem at first glance. Just because you don't see something doesn't mean it's not there. At this minute level of reality, the 'normal' rules of how things work don't apply. It's a world full of surprises and mysteries.

heavily responsible for your overall emotional state as well as your physical health.

6. Meditation improves neuroplasticity (your brain's ability to adapt and rewire) as well as enhancing the connection between the different regions of the brain and physically changing the structure of your brain for the better (aka, neuroanatomy) as well as influencing epigenetics.

7. Quantum effects of meditation on subatomic particles and universal consciousness are being explored. What we know already, though, is that everything is made of energy. So when we align our thoughts and emotions (at a certain frequency) with a desired outcome (at a similar frequency) we will inevitably attract that new reality. We create our own reality.

SOUL WORK:

1. Explore your subconscious by building mindfulness around your emotions during meditation. Keep an emotions diary when you're out and about and see if you can identify what traumas and beliefs they're coming from.

2. Identify your stress triggers and see if you can reduce them for better well-being. For example,

if spending time with certain individuals feels toxic, can you reduce your time with them?

3. Seek professional help if needed for deeper exploration with a trained therapist.
4. If you're ever in doubt about whether you should keep meditating, return to this chapter and remember the tangible, proven effects that meditation has on the brain's functioning and neuroanatomy, as well as its ability to help you manifest the reality you desire.

Chapter 6

The 'MUST-HAVE' of Meditation

"Every morning we are born again. What we do today matters most."

- Buddha.

Once we know all we need to know about meditation, we set ourselves up for intrinsic motivation. That's to say, the knowledge regarding the benefits of the practice piques our curiosity and desire to dive deeply into the meditative world.

In the journey of becoming a badass meditator, overcoming the influence of our environment is the pivotal and critical next step. Before we close our eyes to meditate, we must ensure that our environments, as well as our mindsets, are preparing us for success. Our surroundings, the people we interact with, and the constant distractions in today's fast-paced world can often pull us away from our true selves and prevent us from reaching our full potential on and off the meditation cushion. To realign with our inner essence and tap into our deepest reservoirs of strength and wisdom, we must create the right environment, also known as a 'sacred healing sanctuary.'

A SACRED HEALING SANCTUARY

What does it mean to create a sacred healing sanctuary? It means carving out a space, either physical or mental, where we can disconnect from the outer world and connect with our inner self. It's a space free from external influences, where we can be fully present, fully authentic, and fully ourselves. It's a place where we can strip away the masks we wear in the outside world and embrace our true essence.

A sacred healing sanctuary doesn't have to be a grand temple or an extravagant meditation room. It can be as simple as a cosy corner in your home where you feel comfortable and at peace. It could also be a quiet spot in nature where you can listen to the rustling of leaves and the gentle flow of a nearby stream. To fuel your energy and set the mood further, you may choose to decorate this space with your favourite things – those items that bring you joy and comfort. Add a touch of nature with plants, infuse the air with the soothing aroma of candles or essential oils, and allow the light to be soft. Make sure the temperature is just right for you. Grab all your comfiest cushions and blankets if you're in a cool environment, or switch on the fan if you're feeling too warm. Let the ambience envelop you, creating the perfect atmosphere for meditation.

Allow this special place and any rituals you take beforehand, such as lighting a lamp or candle, to become your daily destination, a sacred, personal retreat to nourish your soul. Here, you can connect with your deepest thoughts, emotions, and insights. Keep a journal and pen handy, so you can capture those profound revelations that arise during your meditation sessions. You may also choose to have a Journaling session before you begin, perhaps writing out your intentions for your meditation or doing a 'brain dump,' on one of the pages, allowing any repetitive thoughts or pressing to-do lists to stay on the page and not distract you too much during the meditation.

In summary, the key is to find a space that resonates with your soul and allows you to feel a sense of serenity and connection.

That said, creating a sacred healing sanctuary is not just about the external environment, rather it's also about you, taking on the identity of a badass meditator.

Imagine another serene sanctuary, a haven of tranquillity, but this time, within you. This quiet, uninterrupted, and cosy psychological space is secluded and private, where you can easily retreat to find peace and calm. Know that, even if you don't have the opportunity to create an outer sacred healing sanctuary, you always have one within you. To help you create this, make sure your body is comfortable so the mind can relax, wearing loose clothing that lets your body breathe freely. This allows you to move and settle into your meditation posture with ease, without any hindrance or restraint.

Then, you're ready to choose your go-to meditation posture. Take a seat with dignity and poise. Sit straight, like the majestic mountain that stands tall and unwavering. Let your neck rise like a graceful tower, while your shoulders gently relax, carrying no burden.

This posture is not about rigidity but about finding the perfect balance between strength and ease. Choose a position that is sustainable, one that allows for relaxation, but not so much relaxation that you fall asleep. Sleeping and meditating are two very different ball games. That said, don't punish yourself if you fall asleep for the first few tries. It's very important to develop a space of non-judgement within yourself, so make sure you're not being too perfectionist with yourself!

It's alright to respond to any discomfort, itch, or pain that may arise. There's no need to suppress or ignore these sensations. Instead, embrace them with compassion, knowing that they are a natural part of the meditation experience.

As you embark on this journey of meditation, preparing your body is like laying the foundation for a soaring skyscraper. It all starts with simple yet essential foundations that prepare you for exponential growth.

Now, let's talk about time. This is something we must be prepared to invest in.

Start by blocking off 10 minutes in your calendar, with the intention to slowly increase this over time to 30 minutes, or as long as you can. For deeper, transcendental meditations, 40 minutes is even better. But for now, start with 10.

Then you must consider when to meditate. You can meditate anytime you want. The best time to meditate, however, tends to be one of three moments:

First Thing in the Morning: Meditating in the morning rides the theta brain wave (the frequency of creativity, on the edge of rest and wakefulness), making it much easier to drop into deep meditation. From theta, you'll move into alpha, the optimal brain wave for relaxed alertness. Meditating in the morning also sets a very positive tone for the day. It helps you start the day with clarity, focus, and a sense of calm.

Just Before Bed: Meditating before bedtime can help relax your mind and body, making it easier to fall asleep and improve sleep quality. It also allows you to release any accumulated stress from the day, promoting a restful night's sleep. At this time, you'll pass through alpha into theta, which will set you up perfectly for falling asleep as well as allowing you to access the subconscious.

During Stressful Moments: Whenever you feel overwhelmed or stressed, taking a short meditation break can help you regain composure and find inner peace. It provides an opportunity to step back from the chaos and gain a fresh perspective on challenging situations. Meditating in these moments acts as a natural medicine in the face of adversity.

Once we have identified the time (or times) we're committing to meditation, we then must forge an unwavering commitment to consistency.

As mentioned in Chapter 2, having a lack of consistency in our meditation practice is one of the top obstacles between us and all the benefits of meditation.

Meditating once per month for three hours is a lot less optimal than meditating every day for just 10 minutes. The same is true of physical exercise. At the end of the day, consistency is king, because the choices we make on a daily basis are what make the difference between a badass meditator and one who dabbles. It's like Aristotle once said: *"We are what we repeatedly do. Excellence, then, is not an act, but a habit."*

Developing a regular meditation practice involves understanding the power of habits and how they shape our decisions and ultimately, our lives. Many of our decisions are guided by subconscious habits that have formed over time, creating well-trodden pathways in our minds. By recognizing this, we can intentionally create new habits, such as meditation, that align with our true desires and aspirations.

The quality of our life is based on our decisions and the quality of our decisions are based on our habits. We might think that we are taking decisions rationally by the logical mind, but most of our decisions are from our involuntary mind, aka, the subconscious.

The subconscious relies on what is imprinted in it through our habitual behaviour. These become subconscious by the formation of deep neural pathways and connections from memorising experiences and habits. These pathways then become automated, such that when subjected to a similar experience, the series of reactions follows without much thought. Our habits create default decisions. We are not living intentionally most of the time but on autopilot. Every such habit develops a neural pathway with the same set of neurochemicals such that it becomes an involuntary action with a known trigger. We live, by default, a rather repetitive life, and most of the time we don't know why we're doing what we do. Therefore, we need to be intentional about habits in our life and make incremental changes to form habits that serve us.

A habit is a behaviour that is repeated enough to become automated. The process of habit formation begins with trial and error. Habits do not restrict freedom, however, they create freedom. Habits reduce cognitive load and free up mental space for free thinking and creativity. Powerful habits, when automated, reduce thinking load and free up space to become more spontaneous. Therefore, if you want to change your results, change your habits.

HABIT LOOP

Understanding the habit loop helps reinforce your meditation practice. First, when creating any new habit, you need a 'trigger,' aka, a reminder, followed by a craving, a response and, finally, a reward.

Here are the basics of this 4-step habit loop (See diagram 6a in the illustrations section of the book):

1. **Trigger:** A cue is needed to initiate a behaviour and consequently, get the ball rolling towards your reward, which is what your body wants. Set up a visible reminder to start a new meditation habit. For example, keep your meditation journal next to your bedside table so you see it as soon as you wake up. Setting an alarm is historically a solid reminder, and is easily accessible on pretty much any phone. If only harsh ringtones are available on your device, consider changing your alarm to your favourite song. You can also set an alarm on Alexa (a virtual assistant developed by Amazon.) My son has developed a routine of asking Alexa to set the alarm to wake him up at 6am. Alexa says, "Sahil, it is 6am. In 5 minutes, your meditation will start." Then Alexa will say again, "Sahil, 1 minute until you start your meditation,' then "15 seconds before starting meditation." So, he gets plenty of reminders for the brain to tune in. If this doesn't resonate with you, you can even stick a note on your bathroom mirror or fridge.

I personally just keep my earbuds on top of my phone on my bedside cabinet which reminds me, as soon as I wake up, to put them in and use my favourite meditation app for a guided session.

If you're struggling with this, you can also integrate your new meditation habit with an existing habit. This is also known as 'habit stacking,' and this can further solidify the practice. By attaching meditation to an established habit, it becomes easier to remember and incorporate into our daily lives. For example, if you take a shower in the morning (hopefully the answer is yes!) you could commit to a short meditation just before you jump in. If you do some kind of exercise in the morning, you can also attach it to the end as a mental cool-down. This works very well with yoga.

2. Craving: Developing a craving for the rewards of meditation, such as inner peace and increased focus, further strengthens the habit loop. The effects of my meditation practice are so strong that I cannot afford to miss out on a single day. My well-being, focus, and resilience depend on it. I feel grounded, calm, focussed and productive all day long when I sit to meditate in the morning. I don't feel tired even after a full day with a hectic schedule. This is the driving force for me to continue to meditate. Identify yours.

3. Response: This is the part where you take action, driven by your craving for bliss! Once you start, the action itself becomes effortless, as your brain has set you up for this expected action, whether you're using a guided meditation on your phone or sitting unguided with a structure in your head.

4. Reward: This is the end goal of every habit. Apart from the usefulness of meditation itself, which can be instant and long-term, I do reward myself with a cup of ginger cinnamon tea after meditation. I know a friend who promises herself a good healthy breakfast after her meditation - the longer the meditation, the heartier the portion size! For my son, simply going in the shower before his older brother gets up is an incentive.

As we respond to the cue by meditating, the action itself becomes easier as time goes on. Establishing a regular routine and committing to it daily can turn meditation into a natural and effortless part of our lives. The reward we experience after meditating, like feeling grounded and at peace, reinforces the habit loop and motivates us to continue.

An additional piece of advice for a smooth habit-creation experience is to set a solid intention. Declaring our commitment to meditation and planning when and where we will meditate, we remove ambiguity and create a specific routine from the get-go.

For example, write a statement in clear bold letters and declare your commitment to the family. Write something along the lines of, 'I AM GOING TO MEDITATE DAILY

FOR 10 MINUTES FOR 21 DAYS TO DEVELOP A LONG-LASTING MEDITATION HABIT FOR MY HEALTH AND WELLBEING. PLEASE SUPPORT ME IN MY MISSION.'. Write it down, put reminders all over the house and give yourself rewards to help you do it regularly.

This is exactly what I did, and I'm delighted to say that my son joined me in my quest. We both meditate first thing in the morning, after writing a short list of what we're grateful for. My son has also increased the timing of his meditation from 5 minutes to 10 minutes, and went on to stack another habit on top of meditation: exercise.

Taking the habit-building process step by step, memorising each action, and celebrating small wins along the way are all part of forming new neural connections in the brain. As we repeat the meditation practice, our brain releases certain chemicals that strengthen these neural pathways, making the habit more automatic and effortless over time.

Joe Dispenza, the author of 'Breaking the Habit of Being Yourself' explains very clearly in his book the importance of small daily actions in building neural connections in our brains. These connections eventually become part of our subconscious and lead to spontaneous actions. Thoughts trigger brain cells to produce chemicals, which then influence our feelings and actions. This interconnected process of thinking, feeling, and being shapes our experiences.

The significance of morning rituals, quality sleep, exercise, and nourishing food should not be underestimated. When combined holistically, they synergistically contribute to achieving a state of bliss.

Looking back, I have realised that I have accomplished something rare. I am exploring my limitless potential and I believe the concepts in this book will help you reach your wellbeing goals like they did for me. We all face challenges in life, and I've had my share of trauma. Fighting against all odds and continuing the practice of meditation, I learnt one critical lesson. Meditation isn't just about sitting still and relaxing. Meditation is working hard for you, and every minute you spend in meditation is very well spent. It is working on your self-image, self-esteem, self-love and self-confidence. It's working on everything that does not serve you, as well as opening doors for growth and new opportunities. So make meditation a habit. With the same habits as we've always had, we will end up with the same results. With better ones, such as meditation, anything is possible.

KEY POINTS:

1. Creating a sacred healing sanctuary filled with beauty and peace will set you up for greatness in meditation. This includes your outer environment as well as your meditator mindset and physical posture.

2. Meditating first thing in the morning or last thing in the evening is optimal. Meditation can also be used medicinally when faced with moments of stress.

3. Following the habit loop process: trigger, craving, response and reward will help you forge new and healthy habits. Once established, they will become automatic and require little effort on your part.

4. Your results are based on your habits. Small behavioural changes compound into big results!

SOUL WORK:

1. Create your sacred healing sanctuary for your meditation, both inside and out.

2. Make sure you give yourself the gift of comfort: wearing loose clothing and supporting your body with cushions and a good posture.
3. 3. Commit to this new habit (clarifying when and for how long you'll meditate) by declaring it to friends and family, and following the 4-step habit loop discussed in this chapter.

Chapter 7

The 'Must-Do' of Meditation

PART 1: PRE-MEDITATION STEPS

"If anything is worth doing, do it with all your heart."

- Buddha.

Now you're well-versed in the must-know and the MUST-HAVE of meditation, you're ready to immerse yourself in the practice itself. Armed with an understanding of the scientific and metaphysical aspects, as well as a committed badass mindset, you are well-prepared to take the next step in your journey.

The 'Must-Do' section is where the magic of meditation truly unfolds. It is the practical application of all that you have learned so far, translating theory into action. By implementing the 'Must-Do' principles, you will unlock the full potential of meditation and experience its profound impact on your life.

The journey begins with three crucial steps that prepare the mind for a profound meditation. They help us release the most urgent and restless energies that might be affecting us in the present moment. By addressing these immediate disturbances, we create a calmer and more focused state of mind, enabling us to delve deeper into meditation.

Once we've released these urgent energies, we create the space and clarity needed to explore the hidden layers within us. These hidden energies might have accumulated over time, from the past day, weeks, or even years, and they can be more subtle and challenging to identify. However, the preparatory steps prepare us to face and work with these deeper issues during meditation. Skipping straight to the meditation practice itself would leave lingering energies, making it difficult to access the deeper and quieter states of mind.

What's remarkable is that when we feel content and at peace after the preparatory steps, we have the opportunity to explore advanced meditation techniques. These techniques can take us even deeper into our minds, facilitating personal transformation and growth. This is where we experience quantum leaps in our understanding and gain the power to manifest our desires and actively co-create our reality.

Once we complete the preparatory steps, we'll delve into eight phases of the meditation itself, building on the foundation we've established. This process allows us to explore the depths of our consciousness, unravel hidden layers, heal past wounds, and ultimately experience the full potential of meditation's transformative power. It's an incredible journey of self-discovery and growth that leads to a more meaningful and fulfilling life.

THE THREE PREPARATORY STEPS OF MEDITATION

Step 1: Pre-Meditation Journaling

Your mind responds to two things, the words you say to yourself and the pictures you make in your head. Empower the mind with words that create the right pictures, and you've set yourself up for greatness in meditation, and in life.

What's more, clearing your mental clutter by putting pen to paper opens your headspace up to allow new thoughts and new states of being to be experienced, as opposed to the old, outdated, auto-pilot stress response. Journaling also allows individuals to gain insights, release emotions, clarify goals, and document their personal journeys. It provides a private and non-judgmental space for self-reflection, self-expression, and personal growth. It serves as a tool for exploring thoughts, feelings, and experiences, and can contribute to enhanced self-awareness, emotional processing, problem-solving, and creativity. The stream of thoughts, feelings, and emotions that emerge during journaling guides our meditation practice and facilitates a deeper and more focused experience.

Journaling, like any practice, can come with its challenges. Some common challenges include finding time for consistent journaling, overcoming self-criticism or perfectionism, and facing resistance to confronting difficult emotions or experiences. It's important to approach journaling with self-compassion and flexibility, allowing yourself to write freely and without judgement. Over time, these challenges can be addressed and overcome through regular practice.

Scientific research on journaling has shown its numerous psychological and emotional benefits. Studies indicate that expressive writing, which includes journaling, can lead to improved emotional well-being, reduced stress levels, enhanced cognitive functioning, and increased self-confidence. Writing about one's thoughts and feelings helps to process and make sense of them, fostering psychological growth and resilience9.

Journaling pre-meditation was actually inspired by my grandfather's wisdom. He never taught me anything about meditation per se, but what he did teach me was that sweeping the floor and cleaning the house first thing in the morning removes negativity, making way for fresh energy. I believe this to be true of the home and the mind. But as opposed to using a dustpan and brush, we use our journals.

Since I started my meditative journey, I have had a strong urge to write. The practice was however very irregular. I only used to write when I found myself in a calm environment, like when I was on holiday. However, therapeutic writing, something I became interested in during the pandemic, gives us the opportunity to consciously move negative energies and create room for more space and clarity. The overwhelming pandemic, the uncertainty of when it was all going to end, the fear

---

[9] Pennebaker, J. W., & Beall, S. K. (1986). Confronting a traumatic event: Toward an understanding of inhibition and disease. Journal of Abnormal Psychology, 95(3), 274-281

of losing loved ones, the news of death, and the lack of resources all loomed over our minds. I found solace in writing, releasing that which burdened my mind. I examined these anxieties and developed strategies to release them, allowing me to regain a sense of control. It was then I learned that writing wasn't just reserved for the good times, rather, it was a limitless resource suitable for use in whichever circumstance I found myself in.

I started by writing one page per day at the same time in the morning. Sometimes, I'd write about all the things I was grateful for. On other tougher occasions, I'd write about the more complex emotions I was feeling and where I thought they came from, using the page to express them in a healthy way. At other times, I'd write about meditation, something I was increasingly becoming more passionate about, or my intentions for the session I was about to begin.

I'd encourage you to begin journaling just before your meditation practice. Whatever ends up flowing from you naturally will help prepare your mind to meditate. Here are a few journaling prompts to get you started.

Gratitude:

The happiest people on earth are the ones who appreciate life's blessings and make time to deliberately celebrate gratitude. Deliberate gratitude is a powerful way to raise vibration and shift your energy. Gratitude journaling leads to increased neurochemicals in the brain, like dopamine, serotonin and oxytocin, the happy chemicals. They train the brain to become more positive and to develop a glass-half-full mindset.

An example of a good gratitude journaling prompt would be to write 5-10 things you're grateful for, like:

- *'I am grateful for the quality time I have with my family every day'*
- *'I am grateful for beautiful summer weather which boosts my mood'*
- *'I am grateful for the food I have in the fridge'*
- *'I am grateful for my parents, and how they help me take care of the kids'*
- *'I am grateful for running water…so many people don't have this'*
- *'I am grateful for my good health that allows me to live life to the max'*
- *'I am grateful for my yoga class that keeps me flexible and fit'*
- *'I am grateful for the birthday cake my sister baked for me'*
- *'I am grateful for all of the magical places I've travelled'*

- *'I am grateful that I'm financially stable'*

  You get the idea. Try and be as specific as you can, and try not to repeat all the same things you're grateful for. Add variety and detail to allow the positive feelings to flow. This will set you up for a very pleasant meditation experience.

Affirmations:

Empower the mind and prepare for meditation by writing down strong powerful affirmative words. These affirmations will create the right pictures, the right beliefs and the right level of confidence in yourself that you'll need to flourish in your meditation practice.

The most pressing emotion can be a source for your daily affirmations. I trace the origin of my emotions, identifying areas that require improvement while reinforcing positive aspects. Affirmations play a crucial role in communicating with the subconscious mind and guiding it toward positive changes. Let me illustrate this with an example:

If I experience anxiety on a particular day, I take a step back to understand its cause. It could be related to various factors like upcoming meetings, potential conflicts, expressing myself confidently, or tackling tasks I'd rather avoid. To address this anxiety, I focus on cultivating qualities like being calm, communicative, clear-headed, aware, and decisive. I repeat affirmations such as "I believe in communicating respectfully and clearly," "I listen actively," "I am confident and assertive," and "I value my opinions and self-image."

Some examples of pre-meditation affirmations include:

1. *"I am a skilled and focused meditator, easily attaining deep levels of tranquillity."*
2. *"With each meditation session, I become more centred and in tune with my inner self."*
3. *"My meditation practice strengthens every day, enhancing my mental clarity and inner peace."*
4. *"I effortlessly let go of distractions during meditation, maintaining a clear and calm mind."*
5. *"As a dedicated meditator, I am open to profound insights and spiritual growth."*
6. *"I embrace meditation as a powerful tool for self-discovery and personal transformation."*
7. *"Meditation comes naturally to me, and I effortlessly find stillness within."*
8. *"Each breath I take during meditation brings a deeper sense of relaxation and presence."*
9. *"I honour my meditation practice, making time for it daily to nurture my well-being."*

10. *"Through meditation, I cultivate a heightened sense of mindfulness and awareness in every aspect of my life."*

Emotional/Brain Dumping:

Journaling about your emotions can be a therapeutic and insightful practice before meditation. It allows you to explore and understand your feelings, gain clarity, and process emotions in a healthy way. A simple, yet effective journaling prompt would be: "Today, I'm feeling..." and then let your pen be your guide.

An example of this would be:

'Today, I am feeling overwhelmed and anxious. The emotions have been building up gradually throughout the week, and today, they seem to have reached a tipping point. I woke up with a knot in my stomach and a racing mind.

I think the main trigger for my anxiety is the upcoming presentation at work. I've been preparing for it diligently, but the fear of public speaking and the pressure to perform well are getting to me. The thought of standing in front of my colleagues, speaking confidently, and answering their questions feels like an insurmountable challenge. But I'm committed to raising my levels of confidence in myself and believe that my meditation practice will support me as I navigate these strong feelings.'

There is no right or wrong way to journal. It is a personal practice that can be adapted based on your individual needs, goals and preferences. Simply commit to the practice and continue to show up with curiosity and compassion, and you will benefit from the insights and growth that journaling brings.

Step 2: Pre-meditation Movement

Once you have journaled, do some form of physical activity. A few minutes is fine. The purpose of incorporating exercise before meditation is to prepare the body and mind for a deeper meditative experience. Exercise helps release restlessness, unblock stagnant energy, and create a state of physical and mental balance. By engaging in physical activity, you can enhance your overall well-being, increase mindfulness, and promote a sense of grounding and presence during meditation.

The combination of exercise and meditation has been practised in various traditions and cultures for centuries. It is rooted in the understanding that the body and mind are interconnected, and by addressing the physical aspect through exercise, one can create a more conducive environment for meditation. Try physically shaking like a wet dog, skipping, walking, running, cardio exercises, yoga, or dancing.. The goal is to release restlessness, promote circulation, and prepare the body and mind for a meditative state.

Step 3: Pre-meditation Deep Breathing

Deep breathing practices have roots in ancient yogic traditions and have been utilised for centuries to harness the power of the breath for physical and mental health. The rationale behind deep breathing before or as you begin meditation lies in the understanding that the breath is intimately connected to our physiological and psychological states. By consciously controlling and expanding the breath, we can influence our nervous system, reduce stress, and create a foundation for deep relaxation and concentration. We continuously breathe in oxygen (prana) and breathe out carbon dioxide into the environment. Most people use only 30 percent of their lung capacity due to their sedentary lifestyle, bad posture, and bad quality of air. Only those who are moderately fit and those who exercise use 50-60% of their lungs. Top athletes can use 90% of their lungs.

Deep breathing optimises the flow of oxygen in the body, stimulates the nervous system, kickstarts physical healing and induces a state of relaxation and focus. Deep breathing techniques help expand lung capacity, activate the parasympathetic nervous system, and promote physical, mental, and emotional well-being. By consciously regulating the breath, one can enhance the meditative experience and cultivate a sense of calmness and clarity.

Deep breathing has physical, mental, emotional, and spiritual benefits. When you slow down the breath, you automatically slow down the mind and the body, making room for inner peace and presence. It's the perfect scene-setter for meditation.

The breath is intimately connected with our mental and emotional state. Our breath influences our thoughts and emotions and vice versa. The breath-emotion loop acts very quickly, just a few minutes of deep breathing can completely shut off your stress response, aka, the fight or flight response.

There are several deep breathing techniques you can try. I'll describe three for you to choose from. I also practise Sudarshan Kriya. Just select one breathing exercise before your meditation practice; there's no need to do all three.

1. **Deep Belly Breathing:** This technique focuses on expanding your diaphragm to achieve deep and calming breaths. Sit or lie down in a comfortable position. Place one hand on your chest and the other on your abdomen. Inhale slowly through your nose, letting your abdomen expand, and feel your diaphragm move downward. Exhale slowly through your mouth, feeling your abdomen contract. Repeat this process for a few minutes, allowing yourself to feel more relaxed and centred.

2. **Box Breathing (Four-Square Breathing):** This technique involves equalizing the length of your inhales, exhales, and breath holds, creating a balanced and soothing rhythm. Start by inhaling through your nose for a count of four. Hold your breath for another count of four. Then, exhale through your mouth for a count of four. Lastly, hold your breath again for a count of four. Repeat this pattern for a few rounds, adjusting the count to a pace that feels comfortable for you.

3. **Alternate Nostril Breathing (Nadi Shodhana):** This yoga breathing technique is known for its balancing and calming effects. Sit in a comfortable position with your spine straight. Using your right thumb, close your right nostril. Inhale deeply and slowly through your left nostril. Once your lungs are filled, close your left nostril with your right ring finger, releasing the right nostril, and exhale through it slowly and completely. Inhale through the right nostril, then close it again, releasing the left nostril to exhale. Continue this cycle, alternating nostrils with each breath. This practice can help reduce stress and promote a sense of balance and tranquillity.

   After practising one of these deep breathing exercises (try them all and see which one works best for you), it's time to transition into your chosen meditation practice.

KEY POINTS:

1. Journaling pre-meditation can put you in a perfectly balanced state to meditate. Gratitude brings joy, affirmations raise your confidence and emotional/brain dumping cleanses your system of lingering negativity.
2. Exercise before meditation helps release restlessness and unblock stagnant energy, creating a more conducive inner environment for meditation.
3. Deep breathing reduces stress, improves heart rate variability, and regulates blood pressure. It has a long-standing history in ancient traditions. This is the perfect pre-meditation activity which is scientifically proven to calm down the mind and the body.

SOUL WORK:

1. Get yourself a journal and a pen, and begin writing before your meditation practice. Choose between gratitude journaling, affirmations or emotional/brain dumping depending on how you feel.

2. Choose a short physical exercise to do just before meditating, such as shaking, jumping or stretching.

3. Try out all three breathing practices: deep belly breathing, box breathing and alternate nostril breathing and see which works best for you. You'll be engaging in this practice as a bridge into deeper states of meditation.

Chapter 8

The 'Must-Do' of Meditation

PART 2: MEDITATION STEPS

"Meditation is not a means to an end. It is both the means and the end."

- Jiddu Krishnamurti

Now you've completed your pre-meditation starter steps, you're ready to tuck into the main course.

By journaling, moving and breathing deeply, you've already slowed down your brain waves, shifting from high beta (and perhaps a bit of stress) to alpha or even theta (emanating calm). As your body relaxed, your mind opened and an altered state of consciousness began to emerge. It is in this state that meditation, and pure magic, begins. There are eight foundational techniques that serve as fundamental elements for any meditation practice, the meditation ladder.

What you're about to learn will take some time to master. Spend a few days on each step before moving on to the next one. As you progress, these steps will merge into a seamless process. It requires time, patience, commitment, and belief to witness gradual change. Remember to jot down any new ideas or insights that arise during the process in your journal.

The effect of meditation does hugely depend on the consistency and quality of meditation you are practising. But the results will be ever-improving and never-ending. Let's dive in.

The eight foundational elements of the meditation ladder are:

Step 1: Breath focus and sense sync.

Step 2: Active physical relaxation.

Step 3: Mental relaxation.

Step 4: Awareness stretching.

Step 5: Running energy and aura cleansing.

Step 6: Grounding and letting go (recognizing, accepting, observing, and surrendering negative emotions).

Step 7: Creative visualisation.

Step 8: Mental rehearsal.

The meditation steps themselves will take you deeper into your mind, encouraging introspection and transformation. Each step will be explained in terms of its purpose and why it's necessary.

Gradually, you can build upon each step until they flow seamlessly together. Just like a habit, program these steps into the subconscious mind such that a mere thought of meditation triggers the subsequent actions in one effortless fluid action. Repeated practice will be associated with change in brain waves, increase in happy chemicals strengthening the neural connections, thereby neuroplasticity and function of the brain.

Steps 1, 2, and 3 focus on aligning your breath, body, and mind. The initial goal is to direct your attention to your breath, relax each body part from head to toe and sync the senses. Following this, shift your focus to the space around your body, its weight, density, and position in the wider space. By concentrating on the breath and physical relaxation, you shift your attention from the analytical conscious mind to the creative subconscious mind, slowing down your brain waves from beta to calming alpha waves. Alpha waves are associated with a relaxed state of mind. Step 3 involves further mental relaxation, slowing down brain waves even more to reach theta states. In these states, you can tap into your subconscious and access higher mental faculties.

Steps 4 and 5 help expand your awareness and maintain the flow of energy generated from the previous steps. They enhance focus, attention, and connection to the present moment.

Step 6 guides you through the process of grounding. You are in a deep state of mind, aware and present after completing the first five steps. You are in a fertile ground for addressing deeply ingrained emotions, blocks, and fears. Understand why they are there and learn how to let go. This step involves consciously recognizing, accepting, observing, and surrendering them. This is the step where transformation or change can happen.

Steps 1 to 6 help in healing and transformation.

Step 7 involves creative visualisation. After clearing the space from negative energies in step 6, you can fill it with new images of who you want to become and what you desire in life. Step 8 is mental rehearsal. Through repeated visualisation of your desired new self, you internalise and manifest it into reality. This process creates new neural connections, chemistry, and pathways that align with your desired reality. Step 7 and 8 help in creating a desired reality.

To begin your meditation, assuming you have already journaled, moved your physical body, and practised one of the breathing techniques, start by chanting "OM" three times. This chant helps you bring in life energy and vibrates the sound into each cell of your body, energising it. See the meditation script in chapter 9.

Step 1: Breath Focus and Sense Sync

We outlined breathing in the 3rd pre-meditation step in the previous chapter. That said, this step differs in that here, we simply become aware of our breathing, with no technique required. After practising either deep belly breathing, box-breathing or alternate nostril breathing, we're ready to drop the structural technique and allow our breath to return to its natural ebb and flow without trying to change it in any way.

The breath is your life force, and bringing awareness to the breath can help you to let go of thoughts or distractions and bring your mind into the present moment. When you are in the moment, you are in the world of possibility. Deep within you, there's a powerful force that brings you to life and cares for you deeply. When your desires align with its intentions, your thoughts match its wisdom, and your passion matches its care for you, it always responds. This force surrounds and permeates you, showing you results from your efforts. Being stronger than your circumstances, surpassing the challenges in your life, and rising above the emotions stored in your body means you're connecting with something divine. Your path ahead is shaped by this collaboration with a higher intelligence. Love yourself sufficiently to embrace this journey.

It is normal for the mind to wander during meditation, but with practice, you can learn to quickly recognise when your thoughts have drifted and gently bring your focus back to the present moment, aka, to the breath. The breath is your anchor to the now. Use your breath to return to the moment and allow your mind to relax, again and again, and again.

Take your power back over your mind and your body with your breath. Bring a balance between the voluntary and involuntary systems, the sympathetic and parasympathetic nervous systems. Shift from fight, freight, and flight to relaxation, restoration, and balance, from high alert to restful alertness, from beta to alpha state.

It all begins by gently observing the breath. By now, after your pre-meditation breathing technique, it should naturally have slowed down a little. If it hasn't, take a few deep breaths into the belly, in through your nose, and out through your nose or mouth. If you're feeling stressed, allow that out-breath to be a sign of relief, letting go of any stress or tension.

As you breathe in, connect with yourself. Connect with what is real. As you exhale, let go. Let yourself relax. Once you can feel a sense of stillness in the mind (or at least more peaceful than before), allow your breathing to become natural, without trying to control it in any way. Notice the temperature of the air as you breathe in and out. Notice the route it takes, from the outside environment to the inside of the nostrils, to the back of the throat, windpipe, lungs and deep at the base of the lungs inside the alveoli.

Allow the breath to provide pauses of pleasure in your mind and body. As you breathe gently and slowly, yet naturally, feel yourself connected to earth's energy. You are breathing, yet the earth is also breathing through you. Breathing in through the nose, the opening point of the body connected to the earth. Exhaling and unwinding any fear. Feel the gift of life fully as you breathe. When you get distracted by thoughts, return to the breath without negative judgement. This is normal. Breathing in, receiving life force energy, breathing out, giving it all back.

Feel the sensations in your body as you breathe; the way the air is cool on the in-breath and warm on the out-breath. The way the belly expands and deflates, as the rest of your body is still and relaxed. This is your sense of feeling, or touch. From here, expand your awareness into your other senses, starting with your sense of hearing. Focus on the sounds around you. Notice any distant sounds, like birds chirping or the wind rustling leaves. Also, pay attention to the sounds that are nearer, like your own breath or the gentle hum of your surroundings.

Now focus on the backs of your eyelids. Even though your eyes are closed, can you see anything in the vast darkness? Can you see any subtle colours or lights?

Now focus on your sense of smell. Breathe in and detect any subtle smells (or not-so-subtle!) in the air. This is where it's nice to have a candle lit or essential oils diffusing as part of your sacred meditation space. Bring your attention to your sense of taste, too. If you brushed your teeth beforehand, taste the minty freshness. If you haven't, be curious about the subtle, natural taste on your tongue.

Feel all your senses together, as best as you can, for a minute or two, all the while, breathing slowly, and naturally.

Practise this entire step for 5-10 minutes initially, without engaging in the other steps. You can set a timer on your phone. As you become more proficient, you can integrate this step into the subsequent ones. Move to the next step when you feel confident in this one. Make a conscious effort to always return to your breathing and your senses when the mind wanders.

Step 2: Active Physical Relaxation

The second step in meditation involves actively relaxing your body from top to toe, noticing any sensations without judgement as you go. We practise body scanning to guide ourselves into the alpha state of mind. It changes the state of mind, from beta to alpha by helping shift your focus from the analytical forebrain to the non-analytical area, the cerebellum. The cerebellum deals with proprioception and spatial awareness (Proprioception is your body's ability to sense its position, movement, and orientation in space without relying on external visual cues). By engaging in physical relaxation, you allow your mind to relax, leading to creative thinking and the emergence of solutions. If you are too analytically concerned, all creative solutions get jammed up. Therefore, actively relaxing in meditation is an important step. It is widely taught but seldom understood. This step aims to bring your breath, body, and mind into total alignment.

Start by noticing the weight of your body, resting fully on the seat or surface you're sitting on. Direct your attention to different parts of your body, relaxing each part one at a time. Start from the head, moving gently to the scalp, the face, the eyebrows, eyelids, and jawline. Make your way down your neck, throat, shoulders, and arms, all the way to your hands and fingers. As you do so, consciously feel the weight of each body part, and imagine sending the natural, calm breath into each area. This will help the area relax. Now make your way through the chest, abdomen, gut and pelvis, releasing any tension or any places you're holding or sucking in. Detect vibrations, tingling sensations, and feelings of warmth caused by circulation in your skin in each of these areas. Release pressures and ligament tension from each part of the body. Now make your way down into your groin, glutes, and legs, travelling through the knees and the calves all the way to the ankles, feet and toes. Relax the body even deeper as you keep breathing.

Observe the spaces around each body part, the volume of space that part of the body occupies in space and its density, letting any tension dissipate. Take deep breaths into any areas of pain, hold your breath, and then let go, all the while without judgement. Try and notice any pain as the sensation it is, without attaching any stories to it. After one body scan, you may feel ready to move on to the next step. I personally recommend repeatedly doing body scans from the top of your head to the tips of your toes and from your toes up to your head again until you feel better physically and emotionally.

Allow the body to fully occupy your attention throughout this step. If you get lost in thought, just gently bring yourself back to the sensations in your body and pick up where you left off. Let the thoughts come and go like clouds.

Practise this step for 5 to 10 minutes initially, starting with step 1 (mindful breathing) once, twice or thrice a day. Once you've practised the first two steps together for a while with success, you're ready to move on to the third step.

Step 3: Mental Relaxation:

The third step in meditation involves achieving mental relaxation through visualisation. By imagining a tranquil place and engaging all five (imaginary) senses while visualising this scene, you can relax your mind and enter deeper states of consciousness.

Mental relaxation helps shift your brain into states of deep balance and heightened awareness, fostering creativity, insight, and intuition. By visualising a tranquil scene and immersing your imaginary senses in it (the brain doesn't know the difference between a real or imagined scene), you can evoke a profound sense of relaxation and engage the subconscious mind. Theta waves, associated with deep relaxation and dream-like consciousness, are connected to creativity, inspiration, intuition, and insights. Insights can manifest as visions, auditory experiences, or sensations during our dreams, or even during our meditation.

Begin by following the previous steps of focusing on your breath and consciously relaxing each part of your body in a body scan.

Then mentally relax by envisioning a tranquil scene, such as a gorgeous, serene beach. Feel the warmth of the golden sand beneath your feet as you take your first step onto the shore. The sand is soft and inviting, moulding itself to the shape of your feet as you walk.

Listen to the gentle symphony of nature around you. The rhythmic sound of waves kissing the shore soothes your senses, while the distant cries of seagulls create a harmonious melody with the ocean's song. Each wave rolls in with a whisper and retreats with a gentle sigh, carrying away any worries you might have brought with you.

As you stroll along the water's edge, the water brushes against your ankles, cool and refreshing. The sea stretches out before you, its expanse a palette of blues and greens that blend seamlessly with the clear sky above. A gentle breeze caresses your skin, carrying with it the subtle scent of salt and seaweed.

If the beach isn't your happy place, consider a woodland walk. Imagine that the air is crisp, carrying the earthy fragrance of fallen leaves and fertile soil. With each step you take, the ground offers a soft cushion of fallen leaves and pine needles, releasing a delicate, woody scent.

Listen intently to the orchestra of nature surrounding you. The breeze gently rustles the leaves, creating a calming harmony, while the distant songs of birds infuse the air with a cheerful melody. The occasional rustling of small creatures adds a playful note to the tranquil symphony.

As you venture deeper into the woods, sunlight filters through the thick canopy above, casting a mosaic of shifting light and shadow on the forest floor. The interplay of illumination and darkness dances around you, evoking a sense of enchantment.

Lose yourself in your tranquil scene, allowing your body and mind to be transported from wherever you actually are, to your natural dream world.

If your mind wanders, gently bring your focus back to your breath, then back to the scene.

The most common blocker I hear from people is that they can't "see" or create a clear enough picture when they try to visualise. That's okay. If this is your case, just make sure you put more energy into the other four senses: the hearing, the smell, the taste and the touch.

As you can observe from these descriptions, there's plenty more to focus on than just what you see, although, if you can use all five senses, please do.

Practise this step for 5 to 10 minutes initially, once, or twice or thrice a day, starting with mindful breathing, then the body scan, and then the visualisation. As you become proficient, feeling the profound effects of your visualisations tangibly, you can merge this step with the next one after slowly allowing the scene to fade away.

Step 4: Awareness Stretching

The fourth step in meditation involves stretching your awareness beyond the physical body and expanding your perception of time and space. Overthinking, which most of us engage with on a regular basis, can hinder our ability to gain a sense of perspective and think clearly.

By observing thoughts and emotions from afar, without getting caught up in them, you gain a greater sense of perspective and reduce the hold negative thoughts or emotions may have on you. Things that used to seem like a big deal no longer have such a strong hold on you. By balancing thinking with non-thinking and focusing on the energetic world, that which lies beyond your body, you can access the answers you seek, recover from adrenal fatigue and promote mental and intuitive clarity. Awareness, after all, can function independently from your body. The body is here and now, but your awareness is not bound by space and time. Your awareness moves everywhere, in the past and future. Your intuition lives in this realm, but it requires deep listening, trust, and patience. Let it come to you, and try not to chase it. Mental clarity and intuition come with sitting still and not overthinking.

There are three ways to utilise your wider awareness: projection, remote viewing, and bringing new insights and information to you. Projection involves bringing your awareness to your thoughts, feelings, and sensations as they arise and simply noticing them without getting entangled. Remote viewing entails observing your thoughts and emotions from a distance, cultivating a detached perspective. Bringing information to you involves recognizing your connection to everything at the subatomic level and allowing answers and insights to come to you for your highest good.

To practise this step, begin by focusing on your breath and reviewing the previous steps of physical relaxation, and mental relaxation. You must be relaxed in order to reap the benefits of this step.

After completing your body scan, play with sending your attention to random parts of the body: the left palm, then the right foot, the left eye and then the pelvis. Observe your thoughts and let them come and go, always returning to your breath as an anchor. Then, stretch your awareness by directing your attention to parts of the body randomly.

Gradually shift your focus from your body to your surroundings. Start by becoming aware of the sounds around you—the distant noises, the subtle sounds in the room, and even the silence between sounds. Imagine that your awareness is like a gentle, expanding sphere that encompasses both your body and the room you are in, followed by the house or building you're in, followed by your street, neighbourhood, city and country. As you breathe, visualise this sphere of awareness growing larger with each inhalation, extending way beyond your physical body.

Imagine that there's no clear boundary between your awareness and the vast space around you in the entire country you're in. Now expand that awareness into your continent, and eventually, the entire world. Feel a sense of interconnectedness with everything in your environment, fostering a feeling of unity and oneness. Stay in this expanded state of awareness for a few minutes or as long as you feel comfortable. If you're feeling adventurous, expand your awareness beyond the planet and into the solar system, into the Milky Way, and into the entire universe. Allow yourself to experience a sense of openness and connection.

Once you've spent a few moments here, transition gradually back into your body. Begin to notice your breath and the physical sensations of your body. Notice how you feel and any insights or sensations that arose during the practice.

Remember that stretching your awareness beyond your body is a skill that takes time and practice to develop. Be patient with yourself and approach the practice with a sense of curiosity and open-mindedness. Over time, you may find that this type of meditation helps you feel more connected, present, and aware of your surroundings, as well as giving you a new-found sense of healthy perspective.

Practise this step for 5 to 10 minutes initially, allowing yourself to observe and receive insights that you may write down in your journal. Once you're able to do mindful breathing, body scans, mental relaxation and awareness-stretching, you're ready to dive into step 5.

Step 5: Energy Running and Aura cleansing:

If everything is made of energy...that includes you! Energy running and aura cleansing are practices that focus on increasing awareness of one's energy field and promoting the flow of positive energy throughout the entire system.

These practices can help in maintaining a balanced energy system, clearing blocks and negativity, and enhancing overall well-being. They aim to bring harmony to the mind, body, and spirit by releasing negative energy and replenishing it with positive, healing energy.

We do this by running energy and awareness through our chakras. Chakras are energy centres within the body that are believed to correspond to specific organs or systems and have specific functions. In various spiritual traditions, these chakras are connected to the five elements: Earth, Water, Fire, Air, and Ether (or Space). They also are visualised with specific colours and sounds.

Here is a brief overview of the seven main chakras:

1. **Root Chakra (Muladhara):** Located at the base of the spine,connected to the Earth element, it represents stability, security, and grounding. It relates to our basic survival needs and provides a foundation for the other chakras.

2. **Sacral Chakra (Svadhisthana):** Located in the lower abdomen, associated with the water element, this chakra is linked to reproductive organs. It is associated with emotions, creativity, and sexuality. It governs our ability to experience pleasure and enjoy life's experiences.

3. **Solar Plexus Chakra (Manipura):** Located in the upper abdomen, connected to the fire element, this chakra is linked to adrenal glands. It is associated with personal power, confidence, and self-esteem. It influences our sense of identity, willpower, and ability to manifest our goals.

4. **Heart Chakra (Anahata):** Located in the centre of the chest and connected to the air element, this chakra is associated with the thymus gland. It

represents love, compassion, and connection. It influences our ability to give and receive love, develop meaningful relationships, and experience inner peace.

5. **Throat Chakra (Vishuddha):** Located in the throat area, connected to ether or space, this chakra is connected to the thyroid gland. It relates to communication, self-expression, and authenticity. It governs our ability to express our thoughts, feelings, and truths clearly and effectively.

6. **Third Eye Chakra (Ajna)**: Located between the eyebrows, this chakra is connected with the pineal gland. It is associated with intuition, perception, and higher consciousness. It enables us to access our inner wisdom, intuition, and insight.

7. **Crown Chakra (Sahasrara):** Located at the top of the head, this chakra is linked to the pituitary gland. It represents spirituality, connection to the divine, and higher states of consciousness. It allows us to experience unity, transcendence, and spiritual enlightenment.

These energy centres play a crucial role in the flow and distribution of energy throughout our body and our aura. When our chakras are balanced and aligned, the energy flows smoothly, resulting in a state of vitality, harmony, and well-being. This balanced energy is often associated with a glowing or radiant aura. Each chakra has its own unique qualities and influences different aspects of our physical, emotional, and spiritual well-being. Balancing and harmonising these energy centres is believed to promote overall health, vitality, and a sense of alignment.

To practise energy running and aura clearing, start by mindfully breathing, then body scanning, then visualising a calming scene, and then stretching your awareness. Please do not attempt to practise energy running without engaging in the previous steps.

Begin the process by visualising a bright, white light surrounding your entire body. Imagine this light as pure, positive energy that is cleansing and healing.

Now Focus on your root chakra, located at the base of your spine. Visualise a spinning wheel of vibrant red energy in this area. See the energy flowing freely, filling you with a sense of stability and groundedness.

Move your attention to the sacral chakra, located below your navel. Visualise a spinning wheel of radiant orange energy. Imagine this energy expanding and radiating warmth and creativity.

Shift your focus to the solar plexus chakra, located in the upper abdomen. Visualise a spinning wheel of vibrant yellow energy. Feel a sense of personal power and confidence emanating from this chakra.

Continue to the heart chakra, located in the centre of your chest. Visualise a spinning wheel of beautiful green or pink energy. Feel love, compassion, and harmony flowing from this chakra

Move up to the throat chakra, located at the base of your throat. Visualise a spinning wheel of bright blue energy. Imagine clear and authentic communication flowing effortlessly from this chakra.

Shift your attention to the third eye chakra, located between your eyebrows. Visualise a spinning wheel of deep indigo energy. Feel a heightened sense of intuition and inner wisdom emanating from this chakra.

Finally, focus on the crown chakra, located at the top of your head. Visualise a spinning wheel of brilliant violet or white energy. Imagine a connection to the divine and a sense of spiritual expansion.

Take a few moments to visualise all your chakras in perfect alignment, with energy flowing freely through each one. See your entire body enveloped in a radiant and vibrant aura that expands from your chakras, creating a bubble of positivity, protection and love around you.

Now, imagine a cord of light extending from the base of your spine, down into the earth. With each exhale, release any negative energy or tension down this cord, allowing it to be absorbed and transformed by the earth.

Once you feel your energy is running clean and your aura is expanded and full of positive energy, bring your awareness back to your natural breath, letting go of the images in your mind's eye. Now your energy is clear, you're ready to ground yourself and let go of any old wounding that's not serving your highest good.

Step 6: Grounding and letting go (recognizing, accepting, observing, and surrendering negative emotions).

Step 6 focuses on grounding and letting go, which involves connecting with the physical world to feel more present and centred and releasing negative emotions to promote self-awareness, self-regulation, and transformation.

In this step we understand that stress is not *who* you are, it is merely a messenger with a story to tell or a warning to share, if only you'd listen.

Emotions are a product of thoughts and experiences. Positive emotions bring high vibe states in our brains, while negative emotions can take a great toll on our brains and bodies. Negative emotions also block the flow of energy thus clouding our awareness and clarity of thinking. If you keep re-experiencing the same emotions repeatedly, your circumstances may not change so easily. This is why I would highly recommend spending time on this step with the intention of becoming comfortable with the process. Your system, as well as your general mental health, will thank you for it.

You cannot create a new future while holding onto an emotion from the past. Recognise and name the emotion. This emotion needs to be unmemorized. Recognising what that emotion feels like in the body and the state of mind that is driven by that emotion is the first step. Admitting it, observing it and surrendering it are the subsequent key steps.

Being present and connected with your emotions is a catalyst for deep healing, uprooting trauma that has been stuck inside our systems for too long, as well as removing the seeds of any new traumas. This is by far the most challenging step, yet it is the key to your greatest transformation. This step must be understood and practised with a lot of patience. Once you master this step, you can enter a world of limitless possibilities. The main aim of this step is to identify the blocks that are keeping you away from your happiest self.

After doing your journaling in the preliminary meditation steps, you'll have set yourself up for success in this one. If you didn't do any Journaling beforehand, you may well get a surprise in this part of the meditation. That's ok. Allow any and all emotions to flow freely.

So in this step, become very aware of what you're feeling, then try and describe it and name it. **Recognise it.** Bring your awareness to the most pressing thought or emotion you're experiencing right now. Deal with one emotion at a time, allowing yourself to be with it and accept it without judgement. Become aware of those physical sensations behind the emotion (does your heart feel fast, does your breathing feel shallow, do you feel hot, jittery, inflamed, inflated, tight, etc). Scan the body and feel into what part you're experiencing an emotion. Is the ball of tension in your stomach anxiety, or worry, or perhaps anger? Is the heaviness in your chest a form of sadness or grief? Is the aching in your neck a form of fear? Now observe your predominant thoughts and feelings around this emotion. Does part of you believe you 'shouldn't' be feeling this way? If you can, allow your judgement to fade away, safe in the knowledge that you're about to take healthy action. You're already taking a healthy action, in fact, just by being aware of how you're feeling. Now, why do you believe you are feeling like this? Explore the origins of the emotion. Do all of this whilst breathing naturally, softly and rhythmically. Don't forget to breathe as you observe your emotional landscape. Own these emotions, any past trauma that arises, and the situations you may have faced as a child.

Don't rush to emotional exits. Be present with your emotion and feel it as energy in your body. Acknowledge it fully. Don't run from it, be with it, name it and explore it. Just observing the feeling and the effect it has on the body will change the feelings itself moment by moment.

Emotions are energy in motion, everything you experience and interact in the external life has an energetic emotion attached to it. Emotions are normal, and should be welcomed. In this part of the exercise, connect to a feeling of **acceptance** around this emotion. You can even say out loud, '[insert emotion], I accept that you are here, and I am ready to allow you to flow through me.' Declaring this loudly throws a spanner into the works of the feeling, like shining light into a dark room–once the darkness is acknowledged, once light is shed upon it, the darkness disappears.

Take your power back by not allowing emotions from the subconscious to fester and repeat themselves. **Observe** the old ways of thinking, feeling and behaving. Separate yourself from the habitual program. Become conscious of those old unconscious behaviours and personalities and observe. With a firm intention, make a choice to no longer want to think, behave and feel the same way. Keep reminding yourself to change the old non-serving ways of thinking, feeling and being.

Here, you can even ask for guidance from a higher power you may believe in, stating

'[God / Universe / Goddess / Great Mother / Great Father, please help me to let go of that which is holding me back from my deepest joy.]'.

No problem can be solved in the same state of consciousness that created it, Einstein once said. So this is where we call on our higher power, our higher self, to release the emotion. This is what it is to **surrender**. Surrendering does not mean giving up. The rose bush surrenders and allows the rose to emerge. When you surrender you allow the next stage of your own unfolding even if you don't know quite what is yet to emerge. You can't both surrender and control the outcome. Give up what you think you know from the limited state of mind, and make room for the new. Make room for the magic.

Trust and surrender to a greater mind, the universal intelligence, the higher power who already has the answers. Let it take your limitation from you. Sincerely ask the infinite mind to resolve the emotion and alchemise it into a greater sense of wisdom. Release your body from the familiar emotional bonds which keep you connected to the past and present reality. Free up your energy. Liberate it from your body and environment. Release it into the earth or into an imaginary black hole.

Practise this step for as long as you need. Take your time, and be patient with yourself. After all, you're becoming conscious of what was once unconscious. This is no small feat. After you've gone through steps 1-5, and then surrendered your emotions to a higher power in step 6, you're ready for step 7.

Step 7: Creative Visualisation

So far, you've learnt how to access altered states by changing brain waves, from beta to alpha to theta by breathing and relaxing physically and mentally. We have expanded our awareness. We have also let go of stuck energy and emotions which were not working to allow new ways of thinking being and acting. Now, we're ready to start realising our dreams through creative visualisation. This differs from step 3, mental relaxation, where we use our mind's eye to immerse ourselves in a tranquil scene. This time, you'll be using your imagination to create a mental video of what you want to achieve or experience. This process is also known as manifestation.

Manifestation involves using meditation techniques to align your thoughts, emotions, and beliefs with your desired outcomes, ultimately bringing them into reality. Some people may be sceptical about the idea of manifestation, and that's okay. Keeping an open mind doesn't mean you have to fully believe in it right away. It simply means being open to learning more about it and considering its potential impact on your life. As we delve deeper into the framework of becoming a badass meditator, we bring the awe-inspiring ritual of manifestation to life; a potent fusion of meditation and intention setting. Here, we allow ourselves to dream big - realism is not welcome here! Go for the most beautiful, ideal, inspiring, and exciting outcome possible. Set lofty goals.

Now, what is the greatest expression of yourself that you can be? How would a great person think and act? How would such an individual live? What does that feel like? By visualising your desired outcome in detail and holding that image in your mind during meditation, you move into a new state of being. You change your energy and broadcast a whole new electromagnetic signature. When you change your energy, you chase your life. You manifest your desires. Let the thought become the experience and let the experience produce an elevated emotion. Let the body believe that the future 'you' is already living now. Remember our chapter on quantum physics? Everything is energy. This is where you match your brain frequency to the frequency of the future you'd love to live in order to attract it to you.

The technique involves using your imagination to create a mental 3D video of what you want to achieve or experience, and simply holding that image in your mind while you meditate. To be able to achieve a new reality or even personality, one must create a new mind and visualise the new version of themselves in creative ways. There are three ingredients needed for creative mental videos or visualisation. First, is to have your **desire** clear in your mind, **believe** it's possible, and **expect** it to happen. This way you're asking the universe to bring this desire to you and put out the signal that you're ready to receive it (because you've already matched your frequency to it, and are feeling all the positive emotions that come with it.) So before you begin this part of the meditation, you must cultivate a burning desire for what you want without wavering. Think carefully about what you want, write it down in detail, make it clearer and clearer and stay with it. Seek the end goal, and don't worry about how you'll get there. If you focus on what you want with passion, you are calling that into existence. We end up attracting the predominant thoughts that we hold in our subconscious. Furthermore, make sure you know the difference between true wanting and immature wanting. Immature wanting is what the world tells us we should want. Rather, go with your unique, inner calling. Your life is a masterpiece, so be the artist.

Having belief in your dream is a very important part of the process. Belief is a very powerful tool. To be it or have it, you must believe it. Believe that it is already yours, and that the universe is orchestrating itself to bring it to you. The wisdom of the East teaches that when you dream in a heightened state of energy during meditation, forces emerge to collaborate with you and make your dreams come true.

Positive self-expectancy brings benefits into the being. Step out of meditation and know that the results are coming towards you. This is called a self-fulfilling prophecy. Think, be and act as if your desire is already a reality. Live the life of that new version of you. Be in the frequency of what you want. Turn fantasy into fact.

Who do you want to be? What life do you want to live? I like carrying out this exercise for the end goals I wish to manifest five years from now. How would this new version of you look? What would they think? Which values would they hold dear? How would they take care of themselves and others? How would they feel? What would their energy be like? What would your new life look like? What job would you have? How much money would you be making? How would your health be? Tailor your visualisation depending on what your most pressing goals are.

As you transition into this step, allow yourself to relax. Imagine that, in front of you, there's a TV screen. You're about to watch the best movie of all time; the movie of your dreams come true. On that screen, watch closely as your goal or dream plays out in front of you. See it, but also feel it (especially if visualising an image isn't your strong point). Feel the joy, the ease, the peace, the love and the sense of achievement. Feel it in your mind and feel it in your body, with every cell of your being. Allow yourself to enjoy this movie for a few minutes as if you're living it right now. Linger here for a few minutes; as long as it feels right. Move into a new state of being. How would you feel if you were this person? You have to feel so much gratitude that your body begins to change ahead of the actual event and accept that the new ideal already is you. Become it. To be empowered - to be free, to be unlimited, to be creative, to be genius, to be divine - that is who you are. Once you feel this way, memorise this feeling; remember this feeling; This is who you really are. Now let go and release it into the field for a moment; just let go.

There are plenty of ways to practise this kind of visualisation. Creative visualisation is a versatile tool that can be adapted to many areas of life. Whether for personal development, healing, success, or creativity, creative visualisation offers a powerful way to harness the mind's potential to create positive change.

Remember to combine **desire, belief, and expectancy** in your creative visualisation. Once you have the hang of this step, and feel comfortable and happy as you visualise your dream come true, make a commitment to practise regularly to shift your mindset and attract positive changes in your life. This technique should also be combined with gratitude for what you already have (which raises your vibration higher), patience and faith, and of course, inspired action. You'll start to receive signs from your higher self on what to do to speed up your manifestation. Be open to receiving them and taking action!

People that use this technique have been able to shift their lives in directions they didn't believe were possible without really understanding how or why it works. I find that to be the most beautiful part of the whole thing – you don't need to understand how it works to benefit from it. Once you're comfortable with this step, you're ready for the final one!

Step 8: Mental Rehearsal

Step 8, much like step 7, is a visualisation rehearsal technique that involves repeatedly embodying desired outcomes or behaviours in your mind. But this time, we're focussing on preparing you for success in a specific event by creating new neural pathways and programming your mind and body for the desired outcome. For example, in step 7, we'd visualise ourselves in the relatively far-off future, running a successful business, whereas in this step, we mentally prepare for an upcoming milestone that will help us get there, like pitching our business idea to the bank this coming Monday in order to get a loan to kick-start the process. Mental rehearsal changes the brain to be ahead of time and to totally prepare for an important event. It develops new circuits, connections and neural pathways that will allow us to carry out what we've rehearsed in meditation, in real life.

Creative visualisation is a mental technique that has been utilised by many successful athletes across various sports. It's a tool that helps athletes harness the power of their minds to improve their focus, build confidence, and mentally prepare for challenges they may encounter during their competitive journey.

Serena Williams, a highly accomplished professional tennis player and winner of multiple Olympic gold medals, openly shares that she used mental rehearsals during meditation to triumph in her matches. Studies have also been carried out on athletes who ran through weight training sessions in their minds as part of their rehearsal. Shockingly, they were found to experience an increase in their muscle mass. And I'm not just talking about their mental image of their bodies during meditation, I'm talking about their physical bodies in the real world![10]

You see, the brain finds it quite difficult to distinguish a real from an imagined scene, especially when combined with a lot of emotion and imaginary sensation. This will create very real-world results. This technique is incredibly useful in the face of adversity, or when challenged to 'perform' in some way on stage or in the office.

---

[10] National Library of medicine, From mental power to muscle power--gaining strength by using the mind https://pubmed.ncbi.nlm.nih.gov/14998709/

The technique is similar to that of step 7, in that you may visualise a screen in front of you from where you'll watch your mental rehearsal movie.

During this final step of your meditation, you'll see the exact images of that which you wish to experience, as well as feeling it all with your five senses. If you have an upcoming presentation at work, how would you want it to go exactly? How engaged are the board? How do you feel? Are you brimming with confidence, and smiling with perfect posture? See it all and feel it all, imagining that everything goes to plan, imagining yourself passing your own expectations.

If you don't have a particularly high-pressure event coming up, you can carry out the same process with your upcoming day. How do you want it to unfold? See your morning, afternoon and evening pan out in a wonderful way. How high is your energy? Can you see yourself and your family smiling? Do you take a wonderful, short walk in nature? Do you take time for self-care, allowing you to feel balanced and healthy? Go wild here and picture your perfect day, engaging all five of your senses.

By consistently practising mental rehearsal with belief and engagement of all your senses, you can create new neural pathways and program your mind and body to succeed in whichever situation you find yourself in.

After completing your mental rehearsal, you've come to the end of your meditation. Slowly bring your awareness back to your body and back to the room you're in. Gently wiggle your fingers and toes, and open your eyes. You did it! You're officially a badass meditator!

Become proficient one step of the ladder at a time. Don't rush. Keep stacking the previous steps to the next one. Once you have mastered all the steps, go with your flow. Some days you might want to spend more time on one step than the other. Use it depending on how you feel.

For example, I focus on grounding myself if my thoughts are overwhelming or if I feel restless. On peaceful days, I visualise my dreams, and on other tougher days, I surrender and seek higher guidance. I start with step one and make my way up the ladder. By repeated practice I have programmed my subconscious, so I go up the ladder effortlessly and linger on the step that I need the most for that day. After a morning dose of meditation, I try to imbibe the practice in my daily routine. I breathe consciously. I use my time consciously. I offer gratitude consciously when I feel good. I ground or let go if I feel anxious, angry, uncertain or if I am in conflict. I try to seek higher guidance for insights or solutions when in challenging situations.

At times if I ever feel that the sequential suggestions are 'a-lot-to-do', I let go and JUST BE! That could happen spontaneously at any time. I Just let go of the following sequence then. I just be in the now and here, in complete stillness and bliss....I have arrived.

KEY POINTS:

1. Meditation begins with the breath – slow down and breathe mindfully to shut off the stress response and turn on relaxation.

2. Then, relax your body further through a thorough body scan from head to toe, letting go of any tension you're holding.

3. Next, visualise a tranquil scene in your head, like a beach or forest. This will induce mental relaxation.

4. Now, expand your awareness by stretching it outside of your body, into the room you're in, into the neighbourhood, country and planet you're on to gain a better sense of perspective.

5. Then, picture your chakras one by one from the base of your spine to the top of your head, allowing the energy to run smoothly. Expand that cleansing into your aura, ensuring there are no blocks or negative vibes in your energy.

6. Next, tune into your emotions and consciously let go of them by recognizing, observing, accepting and surrendering them to a higher power.

7. Now practice a creative visualisation for a dream of yours that you want to manifest. Imagine it's

five years from now, and use all of your senses as you experience it in real time. This way, you attract your desire to you.

8. Finally, do a mental rehearsal for your upcoming day or for an important event you wish to prepare for. This way, you create new neural pathways in your brain to increase the likelihood of success (as you've already practised!)

SOUL WORK:

1. Practise each stage of meditation, starting with mindful breathing, then moving on to body scans, mental relaxations, awareness stretching, energy clearing, grounding your emotions, creatively visualising your dream future and mentally rehearsing for an upcoming event.
2. Solidify what it is that you actually want. What does your dream life look like?
3. Journal after your meditations about your insights.

Chapter 9

Guided Badass Meditation Script

Now you know everything there is to know about all eight steps, it's time to bring them all together and practise.

Once you read this script, feel free to make it your own. Run through it in your head while you meditate, print it off as a reminder or record your own voice speaking it out loud. Use this resource in whichever way resonates with you. Once you practise all steps, they get programmed into your subconscious as a habit and one fluid action.

Sit comfortably, with a tall, straight back, without any rigidity. Let your shoulders drop, and gently close your eyes.

Take a slow, deep breath in, and at the top of the inhale, chant the sound of om. *Om*. Inhale again, and chant the sound of Om. *Om*. Once more, breathe in, and chant *Om*.

Let go. Allow yourself to relax, as you smoothly guide your attention to your breath. Slowly breathing in, slowly breathing out.

[Pause]

Allow your breathing to become natural, now. Notice the

temperature of the air as you breathe in and out. Notice the route the breath takes, from the environment around you, to the inside of the nostrils, to the back of the throat, through the windpipe, and into the lungs, all the way down to the base of the lungs, nourishing the alveoli.

Allow the breath to provide pauses of pleasure in your mind and body. As you breathe gently and slowly, yet naturally, feel yourself completely connected to the earth's energy. You are breathing, yet the earth is also breathing through you. Breathe in and exhale slowly any of the energies that do not serve this moment. Breathe in through your nose, expanding, exhaling through your mouth as a sign of relief, letting go of any stress or tension. Breathing in through your nose pulling all your energies back into your body, back to you. Exhaling a sigh of relief. Breath in deeply uprooting all the stress and tension you have been holding that no longer serves and exhaling slowly softening back into you. Breathe in through your nose giving thanks to everything that serves you, filling your body with new life, new possibilities, making space for what you want. Breathe in and exhale any doubt or lack, unwinding any fear.

[Pause]

If you get distracted by thoughts, return to the breath without negative judgement. This is normal. Breathing in, receiving life force energy, breathing out, giving it all back. Breath in affirming that you are supported and loved. Exhaling through your nose, releasing any shame or doubt. Breathing love into yourself as you inhale, exhaling everything that is out of alignment.

[Pause]

Now feel the sensations in your body as you breathe; the way the air is cool on the in-breath and warm on the out-breath. The way the belly expands and deflates, as the rest of your body is still and relaxed. We're now tuning into your sense of feeling and touch.

[Pause]

From here, expand your awareness into your other senses, starting with your sense of hearing. Focus on the sounds around you. Notice any distant sounds, like birds chirping or the wind rustling leaves. Notice the sounds that are close to you, like your own breath or the gentle hum of your surroundings.

[Pause]

Now bring your focus to the backs of your eyelids. Even though your eyes are closed, can you see anything in the vast darkness? Can you see any subtle colours or lights? Linger here for a few breaths.

[Pause]

Now focus on your sense of smell. Breathe in and smell

your environment. Can you notice any strong or subtle smells? Bring your attention to your sense of taste, too. Are there any flavours you can detect? Be curious about the subtle, natural taste on your tongue.

[Pause]

Feel all your senses together, now. Your sense of touch, hearing, vision, smell and taste, as best as you can. Allow yourself to be enveloped by your senses.

[Pause]

Gently let your attention transition from your senses, to the weight of your body, now resting fully on the seat or surface you're sitting on. Become aware of your body in its entirety. We'll now transition into a body scan. Start from the top of your head, moving your attention to the top of your head. What sensations do you notice?

Moving gently now down the scalp and into the forehead, relaxing the worry lines there, relaxing the eyebrows and the eyelids, feeling them closed and heavy.

Moving now to your nose and mouth, relaxing all of the tiny muscles and fibres around them.

Now, move to your jawline, releasing any tension there, and allowing the bones to be heavy there.

From here, slowly make your way down your neck, throat, and shoulders, feeling the muscles melting like wax, all the way down through both of your arms, all the way to your hands and fingers. Is there any tension here you can soften with your breath?

Now make your way through the chest, abdomen, gut and pelvis, releasing any tension or any places you're holding or sucking in. Detect vibrations, tingling sensations, and feelings of warmth caused by circulation in your skin in each of these areas. If you feel any pain, try not to judge it. Just observe it as another sensation.

Now make your way down into your groin, glutes, and legs, releasing any holding in the quads, travelling through the knees and the calves. As you do so, consciously feel the weight of each muscle group, and imagine sending the natural, calm breath into each area. This will help the area relax.

Now bring your attention all the way to the ankles, feet and toes. Relax the body even deeper as you keep breathing, imagining all the tiny muscles, ligaments and bones of the feet letting go and releasing any micro-tension you may be holding there.

Allow your entire body to fully occupy your attention now. Sense your entire body as a whole for a couple of breaths.

[Pause]

Now we have relaxed the body, we shall relax the mind. You now find yourself standing on the most beautiful beach you've ever seen. Feel the warmth of the golden sand beneath your feet as you take your first step onto the shore. The sand is soft and inviting, moulding itself to the shape of your feet as you walk.

Listen to the gentle symphony of nature around you. The rhythmic sound of waves kissing the shore soothes your senses, while the distant cries of seagulls create a harmonious melody with the ocean's song. Each wave rolls in with a whisper and retreats with a gentle sigh, carrying away your worries.

As you stroll along the water's edge, the water brushes against your ankles, cool and refreshing. The sea stretches out before you, its expanse a palette of blues and greens that blend seamlessly with the clear sky above. A gentle breeze caresses your skin, carrying with it the subtle scent of salt and seaweed.

Linger here, on this beach, for the next few breaths.

[Pause]

Now, return to the present moment. Return to your body. From here, you'll gently stretch your awareness. Play with sending your attention to random parts of the body for a moment: the left palm, then the right foot, the left eye and then the pelvis. Observe your thoughts if they arise, letting them come and go, always returning to your breath as an anchor.

Gradually shift your focus from your body to your surroundings, now. Start by becoming aware of the sounds around you—the distant noises, the subtle sounds in the room, and even the silence between sounds. Imagine that your awareness is like a gentle, expanding sphere that encompasses both your body and the room you are in. Sense the space.

[Pause]

Now stretch your awareness to encompass all of your house or the building you're in. Sense the entire building and everyone in it, including all living things such as tiny fruit flies, small spiders and house plants.

[Pause]

As you breathe, visualise this sphere of awareness growing larger with each inhalation, extending way beyond your physical body, stretching your awareness into your street, your neighbourhood, your city and your country.

Imagine that there's no clear boundary between your awareness and the vast space around you in the entire country you're in. Now expand that awareness into your continent, and eventually, the entire world. Feel a sense of interconnectedness with everything in your environment, fostering a feeling of unity and oneness. Stay in this expanded state of awareness for a few minutes or as long as you feel comfortable. If you're feeling adventurous, expand your awareness beyond the planet and into the solar system, into the Milky Way, and into the entire universe. Allow yourself to experience a sense of openness and connection.

[Pause]

Once you've spent a few moments here, transition gradually back into your body. Begin to notice your breath.

Now we will cleanse your energetic system by working with the chakras; the seven energy centres of your physical body.

To begin, focus now on your root chakra, located at the base of your spine. Visualise a spinning wheel of vibrant red energy in this area. See the energy flowing freely like a spinning wheel, filling you with a sense of stability and groundedness.

[Pause]

Move your attention to the sacral chakra, located below your navel. Visualise a spinning wheel of radiant orange energy. Imagine this energy expanding and radiating warmth and creativity.

[Pause]

Shift your focus now to your solar plexus chakra, located in the upper abdomen. Visualise a spinning wheel of vibrant yellow energy. Feel a sense of personal power and confidence emanating from this chakra.

[Pause]

Continue to the heart chakra, located in the centre of your chest. Visualise a spinning wheel of beautiful light green or soft pink energy. Feel love, compassion, and harmony flowing from this chakra.

[Pause]

Move your focus up now to the throat chakra, located at the base of your throat. Visualise a spinning wheel of bright, sky-blue energy. Imagine clear and authentic communication flowing effortlessly from this chakra.

[Pause]

Shift your attention to the third eye chakra now, located between your eyebrows. Visualise a spinning wheel of deep indigo energy. Feel a heightened sense of intuition and inner wisdom emanating from this chakra.

[Pause]

Finally, bring your focus to the crown chakra, located at the top of your head. Visualise a spinning wheel of brilliant violet or white energy. This chakra opens the door to the spirit world. Imagine a deep connection with the divine through this energy centre.

[Pause]

Take a few moments to visualise all your chakras in perfect alignment, with energy flowing freely through each one. See all seven colours radiating beautifully in unison. See your entire body enveloped in a vibrant aura that expands from your chakras, creating a bubble of positivity, protection and love around you.

Now, imagine a cord of light extending from the base of your spine, all the way down into the earth. With each exhale, release any negative energy or tension down this cord, allowing it to be absorbed and transformed by the earth.

Once you feel your energy is running completely clean and your aura is full of positive energy, bring your awareness back to your natural breath, letting go of the images in your mind's eye. Now your energy is clear, you're ready to ground yourself and let go of any old wounding that's not serving your highest good.

Become aware of your emotional landscape now. Become aware of what you're feeling. Bring your awareness to the most pressing thought or emotion you're experiencing right now. Allow yourself to be with it and accept it without judgement.

[Pause]

Become aware now, of the physical sensations behind the emotion. Does your heart feel fast, does your breathing feel shallow, do you feel heat underneath your skin? Are there any jittery sensations or tightness? Anything, and everything you're feeling is normal. Scan the body and feel into what part of your body you're experiencing the emotion. Is the ball of tension in your stomach anxiety, or worry, or perhaps anger? Is the heaviness in your chest a form of sadness or grief? If you can, name your emotion.

Now observe your predominant thoughts and feelings around this emotion. Does part of you believe you 'shouldn't' be feeling this way? If you can, allow your judgement to fade away, safe in the knowledge that you're taking healthy steps towards complete wellness. Now, why do you believe you are feeling this way? Explore the origins of the emotion. Do all of this whilst breathing naturally, softly and rhythmically. Don't forget to breathe as you observe your emotional landscape.

Be present with your emotion and feel it as energy in your body. Acknowledge it fully. Just observing and acknowledging your emotion will allow it to flow through you and transform.

Now, it's time to surrender this emotion. Say quietly to yourself, 'emotion, I accept that you are here, and I am ready to allow you to flow through me, into the earth's core.'

[Pause]

Ask for guidance from a higher power or your higher self, stating aloud,.

'[God/Universe/Higher Self,

please support me as I let go of that which is holding me back from my deepest joy.]'

[Pause]

Now let it all go, exhaling a sigh of relief, in the knowledge your emotional landscape has been cleansed.

[Pause]

Moving on now, to your creative visualisation. Imagine that, in front of you, there's a TV screen. You're about to watch the best movie of all time; the movie of your dreams come true. On that screen, watch closely as your goal or dream plays out in front of you. Imagine your life five years from now.

[Pause]

See it, but also feel it. Feel the joy, the ease, the peace, the love and the sense of achievement. Feel it in your mind and feel it in your body, with every cell of your being. Move into a new state of being. How would you feel if you were this new version of yourself? Feel so much gratitude now, so much, that your body begins to respond and prepare for this future. Allow yourself to enjoy this movie now. Linger here, and revel in every vivid detail.

[Pause]

Remember this feeling in your heart, in your mind, and in your body.; This is who you really are. Let your energy become entangled with your destiny. [Pause] Now let go and release it into the field, knowing that it's on its way to you.

[Pause]

Now, it's time for the final stage of the meditation: your mental rehearsal. Much like your creative visualisation, see a screen in front of you.

You're about to see the exact images of that which you wish to experience in your upcoming day. Perhaps you have an important event ahead, or perhaps you simply wish to prime your brain, body and spirit for a productive, joyful day. Whatever the upcoming event, now is your time to set yourself up for success. As you carry out your task, how do you wish to feel? How is your task going? As you shine your light, as you become the architect of your day, what are the outcomes you wish to achieve? See it all play out in front of you with faith that it will all unfold in this way, or in an even better, even smoother way.

[Pause]

Are you brimming with confidence today? Are you smiling, holding yourself with a proud posture? Are you taking time for self-care, allowing you to feel balanced and healthy? See it all and feel it all, imagining that everything is going to plan, imagining yourself passing your own expectations.

[Pause]

Now, gently let that go, safe in the knowledge that you've prepared yourself for greatness.

[Pause]

Take a deep breath in, and a deep breath out. Return your awareness back to a new body, to a new environment, to a whole new line of time. Return to the present moment. Gently wiggle your fingers and toes, and now, open your eyes.

[Pause]

You did it. Congratulations for another successful session, badass meditator.

Some guided meditations from Sri Sri Ravi Shankar, Ekhart Tolle and Thich Nhat Hanh may work wonders! You may want to try them. They did work for me.

See you again tomorrow.

Chapter 10

Continuing Your Journey as a Badass Meditator

"Vibration is the language of the universe; align yours with greatness, and miracles will follow."

- Renu Khetan

As you approach the end of this book, another journey is about to begin. We've explored the must-Knows, Must-Haves, and Must-Dos of meditation, and now it's all about sustaining that inner badass meditator within you. And to do that, we must continually raise our vibration. By raising vibration, I'm essentially referring to elevating your personal energy or frequency to a more positive and harmonious state. This concept draws from the idea that everything in the universe, including emotions and thoughts, has a vibrational frequency.

One of the easiest ways to determine whether you are vibrating at a "high frequency", or a "low frequency" is by paying attention to how you physically feel. Do you feel light, energised, clear-headed and healthy? Chances are you have a high vibration.

The main aim of meditation is to increase one's vibration, from mindfulness to transcending the mind, to infinity and beyond! Why would you want a high vibration? The higher your vibration, the better your physical, mental and spiritual health. The higher your vibration, the more likely you are to manifest your dreams. The higher your vibration, the more loving your relationships become. The higher your vibration, the more balanced and happy you are as a human being, with rock-solid resilience to life's challenges. So, what can you do to raise your vibration?

Meditate. Meditate according to the eight phases described in this book, as well as the preparatory steps, and your vibration will continue to raise over time. Each time you sit down to meditate, know that you've become 1% more badass than before and that you're investing time (very well-spent) with the intention of elevating your vibration. With meditation, the sky's the limit when it comes to your personal development.

Your meditation practice, however, and your quest to raise your vibration, can be supported by other simple activities and habits. It's time to think and act holistically. By incorporating positive practices that align with your desires and values, you boost the benefits of your meditation practice, allowing your entire life to become a conscious meditation. Remember, badassery isn't just about isolated moments; it's a way of life. So, let's dive into the seven hidden gems that will help you sustain the habit of meditation and become an unstoppable force in this journey of life.

#1: DECLUTTERING

Decluttering refers to the process of removing unnecessary items from your home and simplifying your living space. The power of decluttering goes beyond just having a tidy home. It's a profound act that can transform your entire life. When you declutter, you release not only physical possessions but also emotional baggage and mental clutter (that may impact your meditation practice). Here's how the power of decluttering can positively impact your well-being and elevate your vibrations:

1. **Reduces Stress and Anxiety:** Clutter can be a source of stress and anxiety, as it can create a feeling of overwhelm and make it difficult to focus. Decluttering can help to create a sense of calm and reduce stress levels.

2. **Increases Productivity:** A cluttered environment can make it difficult to focus and be productive. By decluttering your living space, you can create a more organised and productive environment.

3. **Boosts Creativity:** A cluttered environment can stifle creativity, as it can be difficult to think clearly and come up with new ideas. Decluttering can create a more inspiring environment that can help to boost creativity and productivity.

4. **Saves Time and Money:** When you declutter, you often discover items that you no longer need or use. By getting rid of these items, you can save time and money, as you no longer need to spend time cleaning or organising them, and you can avoid buying unnecessary items in the future.

5. **Improves Physical Health:** Clutter can create an environment that is difficult to clean and maintain, which can lead to the build-up of dust,

dirt, and allergens. By decluttering and creating a more organised and clean-living space, you can improve your physical health and reduce the risk of allergies and respiratory issues.

Here are some top tips to declutter:

1. **Set Clear Goals:** Define the specific areas or rooms you want to declutter and set clear goals for each space. Having a plan will keep you focused and motivated throughout the decluttering process. For example, write in your journal something along the lines of 'Today, my intention is to declutter my wardrobe. This will be completed by 18:00 and I am willing to dedicate two hours of my day to it.'

2. **Start Small:** Tackling a large decluttering project can be overwhelming. Begin with a small area like a drawer, closet, or countertop to build momentum and gain a sense of accomplishment.

3. **Categorise Your Items:** Sort your decluttered items into categories such as "keep," "donate," "sell," and "discard." This will help you make decisions more efficiently and avoid keeping things you no longer need. If you choose to donate your things, you're also benefitting the lives of others as well as your own.

4. **One-In-One-Out Rule:** Adopt the "one-in-one-out" rule, which means for every new item you bring into your home, you let go of one similar item. This helps maintain a clutter-free space in the long run.

5. **Create Designated Spaces:** Assign specific places for frequently used items to avoid clutter from accumulating. Designate spots for keys, mail, shoes, and other everyday items to keep them organised.

6. **Be Ruthless with Sentimental Items:** Sentimental items can be challenging to declutter, but it's essential to be selective. Keep only the most meaningful items that truly bring you joy and let go of the rest.

7. **Digitize Paper Clutter:** Scan important documents and paperwork to reduce paper clutter. Store digital copies on your computer or in the cloud for easy access and organisation.

8. **Clear Countertops and Surfaces:** Keep countertops and surfaces clear of unnecessary items. Only display a few meaningful decorations or essentials to create a clean and tidy look.

9. **Use Storage Solutions:** Invest in storage solutions like bins, baskets, and shelves to keep items

organised and out of sight. Utilise vertical space and under-bed storage for maximum efficiency.

10. **Involve the Family:** If you share your living space with others, involve them in the decluttering process. Encourage everyone to declutter their personal belongings and contribute to the overall tidiness of the home.

11. **Regular Maintenance:** Once you've decluttered, commit to regular maintenance. Spend a few minutes each day tidying up and putting things back in their designated places to prevent clutter from building up again.

Decluttering isn't a one-time task; it's an ongoing process that requires mindfulness and intention. As you continue to declutter and create space in your life, you'll discover the immense power it has to elevate your vibrations and lead you towards a more fulfilling and less complex existence.

#2: HEALTHY EATING:

When it comes to living our best lives, healthy eating plays a pivotal role in enhancing our overall well-being. The benefits of adopting a nutritious diet go beyond just satisfying our hunger; they have a profound impact on both our physical and mental health, as well as our vibration- The modern concept of Gut- Brain Axis. A bidirectional communication between the central and the enteric nervous system, linking emotional and cognitive centres of the brain with peripheral intestinal functions.

The philosophical framework of Rajas, Tamas, and Sattva brings a unique perspective. Rajas, the energetic and passionate quality, can lead to imbalanced eating patterns driven by desires and impulses. Tamas, representing inertia and ignorance, might manifest in unhealthy choices or mindless consumption. However, embracing Sattva, characterised by purity and harmony, offers a transformative approach. Making mindful choices in food, fostering positive communication, and engaging in conscious actions can guide individuals towards Sattva, promoting balanced, nourishing eating habits that harmonise both body and mind. Here's how healthy eating can transform our lives:

1. **Improved physical health:** A healthy diet can help reduce the risk of chronic diseases such as heart disease, stroke, diabetes, and certain types of cancer. It can also improve digestion, boost the immune system, and promote healthy skin and hair.

2. **The Power of Essential Vitamins and Minerals:** Incorporating vital supplements like Vitamin B, Vitamin D, and magnesium into our diet further enhances our physical health. For instance,

Vitamin D facilitates the absorption of calcium, crucial for bone health, while magnesium helps calm the nervous system, leading to restful sleep and the regulation of muscle and nerve function. Additionally, Vitamin B12 plays a significant role in maintaining healthy nerves, blood cells, and DNA.

3. **Better mental health:** The mind and body are deeply intertwined, and our diet has a direct impact on our emotional well-being. Consuming a balanced diet that includes a diverse array of nutrients can positively influence our mood, reduce anxiety and depression, and enhance cognitive function. A healthy gut, which is nurtured by nutritious foods, is increasingly recognized as a critical factor in supporting mental health.

4. **Increased energy:** Healthy eating provides our bodies with the necessary fuel to power through our daily activities and challenges. A diet rich in whole grains, fruits, vegetables, and lean proteins boosts our energy levels, helping us feel invigorated and ready to take on the world. With ample energy, we can tackle our goals with renewed vigour and sustain our stamina throughout the day.

5. **Weight management:** A healthy diet that is rich in whole foods and low in processed foods can help regulate weight and reduce the risk of obesity.

6. **Improved sleep:** Eating a balanced diet can improve sleep quality and duration, which in turn can improve overall health.

7. **A Healthy Gut Microbiome:** The gut microbiome, a collection of trillions of microorganisms in our digestive tract, has been linked to various aspects of health, including digestion, immunity, and mental well-being. A diet high in fibre and probiotics can nurture a healthy gut microbiome, enhancing our body's ability to function optimally.

Here are some steps to help you adopt a healthy eating lifestyle:

1. **Eat a variety of foods:** Aim to eat a wide range of nutrient-dense foods, including fruits, vegetables, whole grains, lean proteins, and healthy fats. This will ensure you get all the necessary vitamins, minerals, and other nutrients your body needs. Eating organic foods and herbs, as they have a higher vibrational frequency, and cutting out processed junk food.

2. **Limit processed foods and added sugars:** Processed foods and added sugars can be high in calories and low in nutrients, which can contribute to weight gain and chronic diseases. Try to limit your intake of these types of foods.

3. **Practice portion control:** Eating too much of any food, even healthy ones, can lead to weight gain. Pay attention to portion sizes and use smaller plates and bowls to help you eat less.

4. **Cook at home more often:** Cooking at home allows you to control the ingredients and cooking methods used, making it easier to eat healthy. Try to cook at home at least a few times a week.

5. **Stay hydrated:** Drinking enough water is important for overall health. Aim to drink at least eight cups of water per day and limit sugary drinks like soda and juice.

6. **Plan:** Plan your meals and snacks ahead of time to ensure you have healthy options available when you're hungry. This can help you avoid making unhealthy food choices out of convenience.

7. **Listen to your body:** Pay attention to how your body feels after eating certain foods. This can help you identify any food sensitivities or intolerances and adjust your diet accordingly.

8. **Eating Satvic foods** includes fresh fruits, vegetables, whole grains, legumes, Nuts and seeds, dairy, herbal teas, honey, spices and water promotes clarity, balance, and spiritual growth.

The power of healthy eating lies in its ability to nourish our bodies and promote overall health and well-being. By making healthy food choices, we can improve our physical and mental health, increase our energy levels, raise our vibration and reduce the risk of chronic diseases.

Remember, healthy eating is a journey, not a destination. Take it one step at a time, and focus on making small, sustainable changes that you can stick to in the long term.

#3: SOUND SLEEP:

This is the most underestimated, underrated habit. Lack of sleep can lead to difficulties in concentration, memory, problem-solving, and overall cognitive function, impairing your ability to think clearly and make decisions. Sleep deprivation is closely linked to mood disorders such as irritability, mood swings, increased stress, anxiety, and even depression, affecting emotional regulation. It also has an effect on weight gain. All of this leads to a drop in our overall vibration. When we do sleep well, however, we enjoy a whole host of benefits:

1. **Improved physical health:** Sleep is important for physical health as it helps the body repair and regenerate tissues, boost the immune system, and regulate hormones that control appetite, metabolism, and blood sugar levels.

2. **Better mental health:** Adequate sleep is important for mental health, as it can help improve mood, reduce stress and anxiety, and enhance cognitive function.

3. **Increased energy:** Getting enough sleep can help boost energy levels, reduce fatigue, and improve endurance.

4. **Better memory and learning**: Sleep plays a crucial role in memory consolidation, which is important for learning and retaining new information.

5. **Improved athletic performance**: Sleep is important for athletic performance, as it can

help improve reaction time, accuracy, and speed.

6. **Reduced risk of chronic diseases:** Chronic sleep deprivation has been linked to an increased risk of chronic diseases such as diabetes, heart disease, and obesity.

The power of sleep lies in its ability to help us recharge and recover physically and mentally. By getting enough quality sleep, we can improve our overall health and well-being and raise our vibration. Furthermore, after a good night's sleep, our morning meditation practice will go much more smoothly!

Here are some powerful practices to improve your sleep:

1. **Stick to a Consistent Sleep Schedule:** Aligning your sleep and wake times, even on weekends, regulates your body's internal clock, promoting more refreshing sleep. Consistency in your sleep schedule optimises the quality and duration of rest, leading to increased daytime alertness.

2. **Create a Relaxing Sleep Environment:** Design your sleep sanctuary to be cool, quiet, and dark. The power of the bedroom environment cannot be underestimated. Don't do anything else in your bed apart from sleeping and making love! Set the Optimal Bedroom

Temperature: Keep your sleep environment at an ideal temperature of approximately 65°F (around 18°C). A cooler room aids in better sleep and helps prevent waking up dehydrated due to excessive warmth.

3. **Invest in Quality Bedding:** The quality of your bed and pillow matters, as theys can alleviate shoulder and neck pain, contributing to a restful night's sleep.

4. **Moderate Liquid Intake Before Bedtime:** Limit your liquid intake close to bedtime to avoid disturbances from frequent trips to the bathroom during the night.

5. **Unplug from Electronic Devices:** The blue light emitted by electronic devices disrupts the production of sleep-inducing melatonin. Minimise electronic device usage at least an hour before bedtime. Wear blue-light-blocking glasses 90 minutes before bed if you're watching a movie/are obliged to use your devices.

6. **Harness the Power of Supplements:** Consider incorporating ginkgo before sleep, known for its calming properties, and a lavender scent diffuser to promote relaxation and deeper sleep.

7. **Steer Clear of Stimulants:** Avoid consuming caffeine, nicotine, and alcohol in the evening, as they can interfere with falling asleep and disrupt sleep patterns. If you're a coffee drinker, consider having your last cup by 2pm, or going for decaf.

8. **Embrace Regular Exercise:** Engage in regular physical activity, but avoid exercising close to bedtime, as it can be stimulating. Morning outdoor activities, such as sun salutations, expose you to natural light, further supporting a healthy sleep-wake cycle.

9. **Establish a Tranquil Bedtime Routine:** Wind down with a soothing bedtime ritual, signalling your body that it's time to sleep. Indulge in a warm bath, read a book, or practise relaxation techniques like deep breathing or meditation.

10. **Nap Wisely:** Limit daytime naps to 20-30 minutes, and avoid napping later in the day if you experience difficulty falling asleep at night.

11. **Consider sleeping keeping your head towards south** (east-west - second best option) but never north.

Remember, each person's sleep needs are unique, so listen to your body and adjust these habits as needed. If sleep troubles persist, seek guidance from a healthcare professional to rule out any underlying sleep disorders or medical conditions. By nurturing positive sleep habits, you raise your vibration, allowing you to embrace each day with renewed energy and vitality.

#4: COMMUNITY:

Community is a fundamental human need that is pivotal when it comes to living a healthy life and forging a high vibration. Studies are beginning to emerge on the topic that proves this, linking a sense of community with longevity[11]. Moreover, having a community provides:

1. **Belonging and Identity:** Community fulfils our innate need for a sense of belonging and shared identity, offering a place where we feel accepted and valued.

2. **Emotional Support:** Communities provide social interactions that reduce feelings of isolation and loneliness, offering emotional

---

[11] National Library of Medicine, Social relationships and physiological determinants of longevity across the human life span https://www.ncbi.nlm.nih.gov/pmc/articles/PMC4725506/

support and connections that enhance overall well-being.

3. **Knowledge and Resources:** Through community interactions, we exchange knowledge, experiences, and resources, contributing to personal growth and the collective advancement of skills and opportunities.

4. **Collective Growth:** Communities foster collaboration and shared learning, enabling individuals to thrive together and overcome challenges through collective effort.

5. **Resilience and Assistance:** During difficult times, communities offer a network of assistance, empathy, and understanding, enhancing our resilience and ability to cope with adversity.

6. **Cultural Diversity:** Communities encompass diverse perspectives, cultures, and backgrounds, enriching our understanding of the world and promoting a broader worldview.

7. **Shared Purpose:** Being part of a community provides a sense of shared purpose and common goals, contributing to a greater sense of meaning and fulfilment in our lives.

The concept of raising one's vibration, or increasing one's positive energy and spiritual awareness, is often associated with the idea of community, or coming together with others who share similar beliefs and goals. Your community could be your colleagues, the friends you already have, your family, and your partner. Your community can always be expanded. Before you begin looking for a like-minded community, or nurturing one you already have, be sure to cut out toxic, low-vibrational people from your life that weigh you down. If being around them makes you feel heavy, stressed and negative, it may be time to let them go. After all, if they're holding you back from your happiest self, what's the point in the relationship in the first place?

When individuals focus on positivity and higher energy levels, this positive energy can be contagious and spread throughout a community. This is why it is often said that communities can play a powerful role in raising the vibrations of individuals within them.

Here are some steps that can be taken to build a powerful community to raise the collective vibration:

1. **Identify the shared goals and values:** For individuals to come together and build a powerful community, it is important to have a shared vision and values that guide their actions. This could be achieving inner peace, promoting positive mental health, or increasing self-

awareness. Identifying these shared goals will help give direction to the community and create a sense of unity.

2. **Establish regular meetups:** Communities thrive when there is consistent interaction among the members. Establishing regular meetups could be in person or online. The meetups could involve group meditations, yoga, book clubs, or workshops. Participating in these regular group activities can help reinforce the community's shared vision and create a sense of belonging among the members.

3. **Encourage open communication:** Open communication is essential for building trust and creating a sense of psychological safety in the community. Encourage members to share their thoughts, feelings, and experiences openly with each other. Create a safe space where members can share their challenges and receive support and guidance from other members.

4. **Practice gratitude:** Gratitude is a powerful tool that can help elevate vibrations. Encourage members of the community to embrace an attitude of gratitude by celebrating each other's successes and appreciating the daily blessings.

5. **Foster a culture of service:** Serving others is a great way to practice kindness and generosity,

which can elevate vibrations. Encourage members of the community to give back to society through volunteering or community service projects.

6. **Celebrate diversity:** Embrace the diversity of the community by creating an inclusive environment that accepts different belief systems, cultures, and backgrounds.

A community can be formed that promotes positive vibrations and supports its members in achieving personal growth and well-being. If you haven't found it yet, go out there and create your own! Join a yoga class, art class, dancing class, gaming group, walking group or any pre-existing community in your area to get started.

#5: MOVEMENT AND SWEATING:

The power of sweat cannot be berated. Sweating is a natural bodily function that allows us to regulate our body temperature, but it has also been found to have other benefits, including the ability to raise our vibration. Sweating helps to remove toxins from your body, which cleanses the system, improves mental clarity and boosts energy levels. Many ancient cultures around the world engage in sweating rituals, such as sauna or sweat lodge ceremonies, to cleanse the body and elevate spiritual awareness. These traditions involve heating up a small space to high temperatures and sweating profusely. This process can help to detoxify the body and promote a deeper spiritual connection, leading to an elevated state of consciousness.

In addition, physical exercise has been found to release endorphins, which are feel-good hormones that can promote positive emotions and elevate vibrations. This is why physical activities such as yoga, running, and dance can be such effective ways of raising our vibration.

Here are steps that can be taken to sweat and raise your vibration:

1. **Engage in physical exercise:** One of the best ways to sweat and raise vibration is through physical exercise. Activities such as running, dancing, or other forms of cardio can help to raise your heart rate and make you sweat. Try to find a form of exercise that you enjoy so that it feels less like a chore and more like an opportunity to release stress and tension.

2. **Incorporate meditation or mindfulness:** Another way to raise vibrations while sweating is to incorporate meditation or mindfulness into your exercise routine. Try to focus on the present moment and connect with your breath while you exercise, rather than getting caught up in your thoughts. This can help to promote a sense of relaxation and inner peace.

3. **Take a hot bath or sauna:** Another way to promote sweating is by taking a hot bath (with Epsom salts is

ideal, due to the magnesium content) or visiting a sauna. The heat can help to increase circulation and promote sweating, which can help to release toxins from the body and elevate vibrations. Just remember to stay hydrated before and after.

4. Engage in traditional sweating rituals: Many cultures around the world have traditional rituals involving sweating, such as sweat lodges or steam rooms. If you can participate in one of these rituals, it can be a powerful way to connect with your body, mind and spirit and raise your vibrations.

5. Stay hydrated: No matter how you choose to sweat, it is important to stay hydrated. Drink plenty of water before, during, and after sweating to ensure that your body functions at its optimal level.

By following these steps, you can incorporate sweating into your daily routine to release toxins, elevate endorphins, promote relaxation and inner peace, and ultimately raise your vibration.

#6: NATURE:

Being in nature offers a wide array of benefits. Remember how we use natural, tranquil scenes in our meditation practice? Being in nature physically, just like imagining we're there in our mind's eye has a whole host of surprising benefits for your vibration:

1. **Stress Reduction:** Spending time in natural settings can lower cortisol levels and reduce stress, promoting a calmer and more relaxed state of mind.

2. **Improved Mood:** Nature has a positive impact on mood, alleviating feelings of anxiety and depression and promoting a sense of happiness and well-being.

3. **Enhanced Creativity:** Immersing oneself in natural environments can stimulate creative thinking and problem-solving abilities.

4. **Increased Physical Activity:** Outdoor activities in nature, such as hiking, biking, or simply walking, encourage physical movement and exercise, improving cardiovascular health and overall fitness.

5. **Better Cognitive Function:** Nature exposure has been linked to improved attention, focus, and cognitive performance.

6. **Boosted Immune System: Phytoncides** released by trees and plants in forests have been shown to enhance the activity of immune cells, contributing to a stronger immune system.

7. **Restored Mental Fatigue:** Nature provides a mental reprieve from the demands of modern life,

helping to restore mental energy and alleviate mental fatigue.

8. **Connection to the Present Moment:** Being in nature encourages mindfulness and being present, fostering a deeper connection to the current moment and a sense of grounding.

9. **Improved Sleep:** Exposure to natural light and fresh air can positively impact sleep patterns, leading to better quality sleep (as mentioned earlier).

10. **Reduced Blood Pressure:** Spending time in nature has been associated with lower blood pressure levels, contributing to cardiovascular health.

11. **Enhanced Respiratory Health:** Cleaner air in natural settings can improve respiratory function and lung health.

12. **Increased Vitamin D Intake:** Outdoor time in the sun helps the body produce vitamin D, which is essential for bone health and overall well-being.

13. **Connection to the Earth:** Being in nature fosters a sense of connectedness to the environment and a greater appreciation for the natural world.

14. **Sense of Awe and Wonder:** Nature's beauty and vastness inspire feelings of awe and wonder, encouraging a broader perspective on life.

In a nutshell, the benefits of being in nature extend across physical, mental, and emotional domains, offering a holistic approach to improving well-being and quality of life. How do you do it...well...get outside! No matter where you are in the world, your unique natural landscape is awaiting you. Whether you're close to a beach, forest, mountain, jungle, desert, volcano, fjord, waterfall, rise terrace or lake, make a commitment to spending some time there. Live in London, Paris, New York, or a huge city far away from any of this? Then find your local park.

#7: GRATITUDE:

Last but certainly not least, is the act of appreciation. Practising gratitude is a hidden superpower and one of the most effective ways to raise your vibration at any moment of the day. It is the key to happiness, and offers a multitude of psychological, emotional, and social benefits that contribute to overall well-being back by science:

1. **Improved Mental Health: Regular** gratitude practice has been linked to reduced symptoms of depression, anxiety, and stress, promoting a more positive mindset. Gratitude cultivates positive emotions like joy, contentment, and happiness, fostering an optimistic outlook on life.

2. **Better Self-Esteem:** Recognizing and acknowledging one's blessings can boost self-esteem and self-worth, enhancing overall self-perception.

3. **Reduced Materialism:** Gratitude shifts the focus from what you don't have to what you do have, reducing the longing for material possessions to 'fill the void.' By focusing on what one has rather than what is lacking, gratitude promotes a sense of satisfaction with life and promotes contentment.

4. **Lowered Blood Pressure:** Some studies suggest that regular gratitude practice may contribute to lower blood pressure and improved heart health.

5. **Mindfulness and Present Moment Awareness:** Gratitude encourages individuals to be present and mindful, appreciating the here and now.

Practising gratitude involves actively acknowledging and appreciating the positive aspects of your life. Here's how to incorporate gratitude into your daily routine:

1. **Keep a Gratitude Journal:** Set aside a few minutes each day to write down things you're grateful for. Do this straight away in the morning before you meditate. Reflect on moments, people, experiences, or even small blessings.

2. **Express Appreciation:** Tell someone you're grateful for them or their actions. A sincere "thank you" can create meaningful connections.
3. **Visual Reminders:** Place a gratitude-related quote or image somewhere you'll see it daily as a gentle reminder.
4. **Appreciate Challenges:** Find silver linings in difficult situations. Consider what you've learned or how you've grown from challenges.
5. **Shift Your Language:** Replace complaining with expressions of gratitude. Instead of saying "I have to," say "I get to."
6. **Gratitude Walk:** During a nature walk, focus on the beauty around you and reflect on the things you're thankful for.
7. **Pause Before Meals:** Before eating, take a moment to express gratitude for the nourishment you're about to receive.

By incorporating gratitude into your everyday routine, it will transform from a habit into a part of who you are. And when gratitude is part of who you are, joy is too! The benefits of gratitude truly are endless, and many books have been written on the subject with emerging scientific evidence that gratitude truly is the key to unlocking joy and satisfaction within the human brain. If you take away anything from this section, let it be this.

KEY POINTS:

1. Meditation aims to raise our vibration.

2. As well as meditating daily, embrace a holistic approach to raising your vibration by incorporating positive practices aligned with your values.

3. Decluttering goes beyond tidying up; it releases emotional and mental baggage, reduces stress, and enhances well-being.

4. A nutritious diet enhances physical and mental health, increases energy, aids weight management, and promotes better sleep.

5. Quality sleep repairs the body, improves mental health, increases energy, and enhances memory and learning.

6. A loving community of positive, like-minded individuals fosters deep physical and emotional wellbeing, filling our life with a sense of meaning.

7. Sweating through physical exercise or traditional rituals helps release toxins, elevate endorphins, and raise vibration.

8. Getting out into nature calms down the stress response and promotes a sense of awe and inner peace.

9. Keeping a gratitude journal or simply being more grateful throughout the day is the key to unlocking our deepest joy.

SOUL WORK:

Set an intention to practise all of these vibration-raising activities in your calendar over the next month, and write down how you're feeling afterwards. I promise it will be the most pleasurable experiment you've ever done!

Chapter 11

Final Word

"Find your inner badass through meditation; it's not just a practice, it's a way of life."

- Renu Khetan

As we approach the final chapter of this book, I want to leave you with a powerful message, one that encapsulates the essence of what we've explored together.

So, my dear reader, remember that you're a meditation badass now. And to stay that way, stay committed and consistent on your journey. You hold within you the keys to unlock your true potential.

Fuel your meditation practice with a burning desire to deepen your inner peace, cultivate compassion, or attain wisdom. Let this fiery passion propel you forward on your journey. Cultivate faith in your meditation practice, trusting in its potential to bring about positive change in your life, relationships, and self-awareness.

Make the decision to prioritise meditation in your life, committing to regular practice to nurture mindfulness, emotional balance, and well-being. Create a dedicated space, set a regular practice schedule, and incorporate meditation into your daily life to make the most of its transformative benefits. Make it non-negotiable.

Embrace positive affirmations and intentions during meditation to reinforce self-compassion, self-healing, and positive mental states. Utilise meditation to transmute negative emotions and mental states into positive energy through mindfulness, acceptance, and compassionate self-inquiry. This leads to emotional healing and personal growth.

Harness the power of imagination during meditation by visualising peaceful scenes, cultivating positive mental images, and creatively engaging with the practice.

Engage with meditation communities, retreats, or group practices to foster a supportive environment where insights are shared, progress is supported, and understanding is deepened together.

I hope from the bottom of my heart that you continue to give yourself the gift of meditation, and that it becomes part of your identity. Because knowledge alone is not enough. Although it's amazing you read this book, it's now time to step into action, do the work and apply the principles.

This book has been a roadmap, guiding you to heal, transform, and change your reality. In this modern age, we have the extraordinary ability to create a quantum leap towards our goals and desires. The universe awaits your command, ready to align with your focused intention.

Now, my part is done, and yours begins. Embrace your unique journey, armed with newfound knowledge and a burning desire for success. The path may not always be smooth, but remember, setbacks are merely stepping stones to greatness. So, go forth, and achieve with fervour through meditation. Your dreams are within reach, waiting for you to claim them. The world needs your brilliance, and your unique contribution. The world needs you to be your happiest self.

Dive into meditation, and emerge as a badass; it's the ultimate life hack for success and fulfilment.

With gratitude for joining me on this journey, and from my heart to yours,

Namaste, fellow badass!

What a transformation divine!

From a creeping caterpillar shy.

Spinning into a chrysalis,

to an uplifting, free butterfly.

Ah! The flying flowers,

Eternal love with the bloom,

Flitting and fluttering,

a butterfly spring is soon.

Oh, flutterby! Reach high,

with hope to touch the sun,

and kiss the infinite sky.

A gift of a crooked fly.

An existence so charismatic.

Butterfly Charisma'

- **Renu khetan**

Illustrations

2A. MEDITATION LADDER

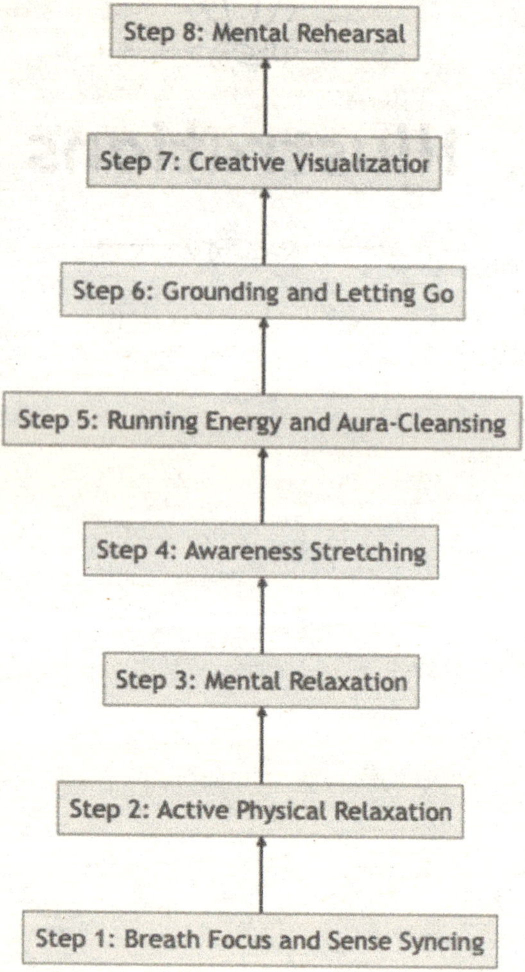

2B. MEDITATION LADDER, SHOWING THE PROGRESSION FROM STEP 1 TO STEP 8, ALONG WITH THE SPECIFIC ACTIONS OR STATES THAT EACH STEP LEADS TO

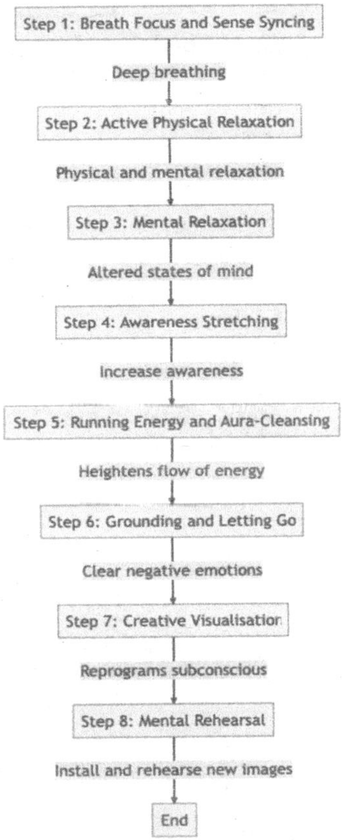

3A. WHO IS A BADASS MEDITATOR?

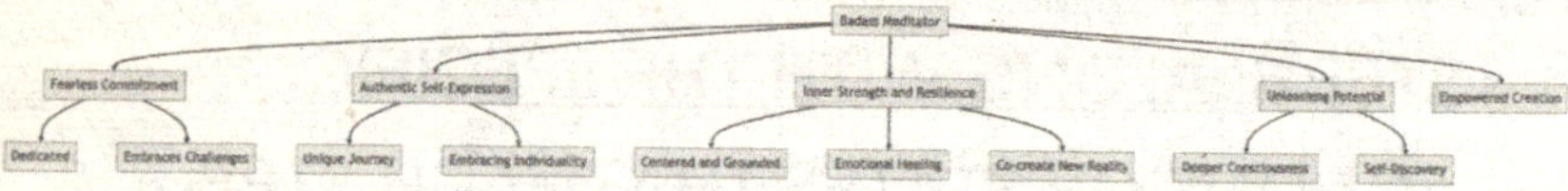

5A. MIND BRAIN BODY CONNECTION

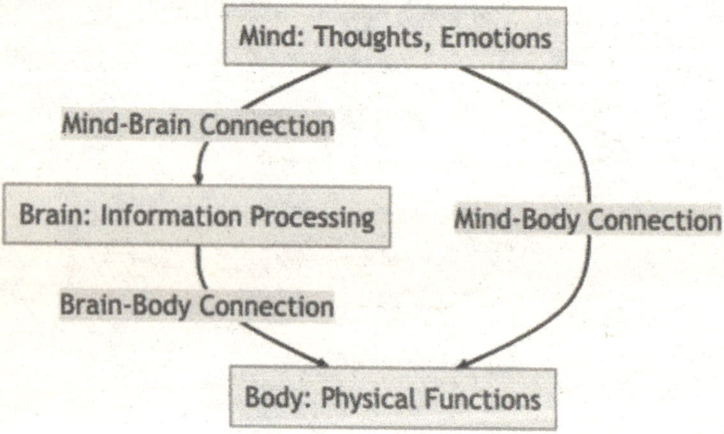

5B. BRAIN WAVES AND STATES OF MIND

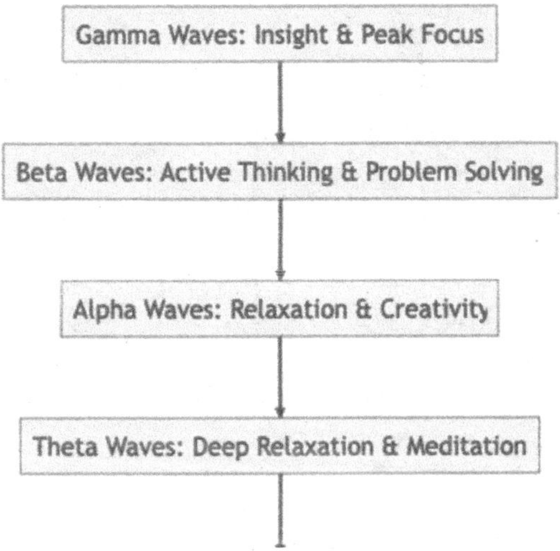

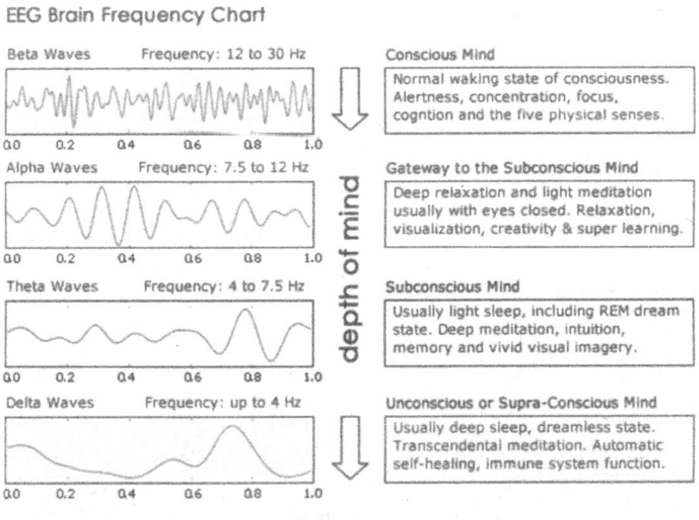

6a. Habit loop

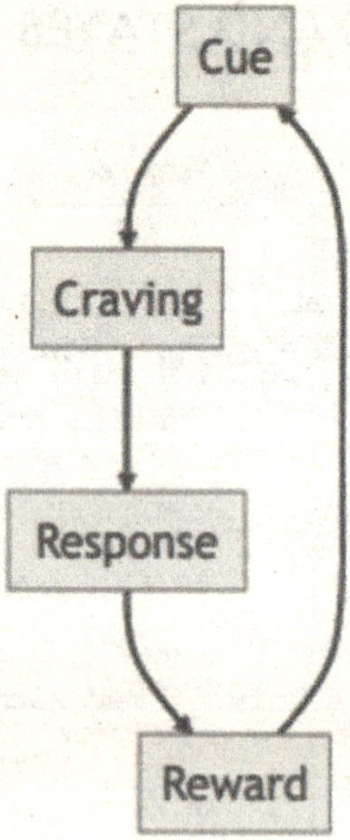

MY DAILY MEDITATION RITUAL

THE GOLDEN HOUR

6:00 AM - Wake with Intention:

• Greet the day with a smile, stretch joyfully, and articulate your intention.

• Take a moment to express gratitude for the new beginning.

6:10 AM - Pre meditation steps:

• **Journaling (5 minutes):**

◦ Make a gratitude list of 10 things, write 5 affirmations, or something that inspires you today. Writing your most pressing emotion.

• **Gentle Exercise (5 minutes):**

◦ Practice Energy dance, Tai Chi or mindful stretching to connect with your body.

• **Deep Breathing (5 minutes):**

◦ Explore the alternate nasal breathing technique to initiate relaxation.

6:30 AM - Meditation - Journey Up the Meditation Ladder:

• **Step 1: Breathe and sense sync (2 minutes):**

• **Step 2: Physical Awareness (2 minutes):**

• **Step 3: Mental Clarity (2 minutes):**

• **Step 4: Stretch Awareness (2 minutes):**

• **Step 5: Energy Run and Aura Clearing (2 minutes):**

• **Step 6: Grounding (2 minutes):**

• **Step 7: Focused Visualisation (2 minutes):**

• **Level 8: Mental Rehearsal (2 minutes):**

****6:50 AM - Final Reflection:****

• Rest your hands over your heart, feeling inner warmth.

• Thank yourself for this sacred time, and carry serenity with you.

Note:

• Tailor this routine to resonate with your unique needs and daily rhythm.

• Consider adding soothing music or nature sounds to enhance the ambiance.

Thank Yous

A Symphony of Gratitude –

A Heartfelt Thanks to the Universe and You

When I embarked on this journey, it was a solitary dance between me, my baby (this book), and the divine whisper of inspiration. But as the path unfolded, it became a symphony, filled with the melody of wonderful souls who joined me, supported me, and breathed life into this dream. I always believed that my goal was so meaningful that the Universe would guide me, and it did, in ways more profound and beautiful than I could have ever imagined.

To the Universe, my eternal guide, thank you for having my back, for orchestrating this dance, for the people, the chances, the answers, the support, and the time. You

were the unseen hand, the silent composer, the magic behind it all.

To my parents, the roots of my being, the pillars of love and wisdom, thank you for nurturing me, for your unwavering faith, for the values you instilled, and the endless support you've given. Your blessings have been my guiding star.

To my husband, Achal, the first ray of sunshine every morning, the silent strength, the forceful support, my biggest cheerleader - thank you for being the wind beneath my wings.

To my children, Adit and Sahil, my endless wellspring of love, joy, and inspiration, thank you for the hugs, the cuddles, the laughter, and for being the beautiful souls you are.

To my brother, Umesh, my biggest inspiration, motivator, and life coach, thank you for introducing meditation into my life and igniting the fire that continues to burn. Your wisdom and guidance have been a beacon on this journey.

To my sister, Hema, who saw my worth before I could, who believed in me when I doubted, thank you for being my rock.

To my tech-savvy nephew, Arnav, thank you for adding your techy flavour, for being my mainstay, and for your

invaluable assistance in completing this book. Your youthful energy and expertise have been a driving force.

To my family, Aishwarya and Nandan, friends, supporters, who contributed, promoted, and stood by me, thank you for being part of this collective effort, this beautiful tapestry.

To Amy, more than an editor, a friend, a confidante, a brilliant mind, thank you for being the first to love my book, for your kindness, your humour, your unwavering support.

To the publishing team, Aruna, Merril and Debdatta, my gratitude for your hard work, dedication, and belief in this project.

To Sri Sri Ravishankar, Vishen Lakhiani, Bob Proctor, Joe Dispenza, James Clear, and Kristina Mand, I extend my profound gratitude. Your teachings, insights, and pioneering work have been the reason behind this book. You have been the storehouse of knowledge that I have been soaking in, and your influence has shaped my thoughts and guided my pen.

And finally, to you, dear reader, the heartbeat of this book, the reason it's alive, thank you for holding it in your hands, for giving it a home in your heart. A book becomes real when it finds its reader, and you have made this dream a reality.

In the pages of this book, you'll find pieces of my soul, echoes of the love and support I've received, and a testament to the power of faith, perseverance, and human connection. Thank you for being part of this journey, for making it meaningful, for being the melody in this symphony of gratitude.

With all my heart,

Renu Khetan

Special Bonuses

HERE'S HOW TO ACCESS

THE ***Special Bonuses***

THAT COME WITH THIS BOOK

Don't miss these essential tools! To get bonus materials, including free guided meditation and the companion workbook to this book, scan the QR code or visit www.badassmeditator.org

QR code for workbook and guided meditation